THEOLOGY FOR THE REST OF US

BOOKS BY LISA HARPER

A Jesus-Shaped Life
Theology for the Rest of Us

THEOLOGY FOR THE REST OF US

A User-Friendly Guide to Super Cool, Really Transformational Stuff About God and Why It Matters

LISA HARPER

Revell
a division of Baker Publishing Group
Grand Rapids, Michigan

Published by Revell
a division of Baker Publishing Group
Grand Rapids, Michigan
RevellBooks.com

Printed in China

Library of Congress Cataloging-in-Publication Data
Names: Harper, Lisa, 1963– author
Title: Theology for the rest of us : a user-friendly guide to super cool, really transformational stuff about God and why it matters / Lisa Harper.
Description: Grand Rapids, Michigan : Revell, a division of Baker Publishing Group, [2026] | Includes bibliographical references.
Identifiers: LCCN 2025048661 | ISBN 9780800744786 cloth | ISBN 9781493454068 ebook
Subjects: LCSH: Theology, Practical | Christian life
Classification: LCC BV3 .H336 2026
LC record available at https://lccn.loc.gov/2025048661

Cover design by Laura Klynstra

The author is represented by Alive Literary Agency, www.aliveliterary.com.

Baker Publishing Group publications use paper produced from sustainable forestry practices and postconsumer waste whenever possible.

26 27 28 29 30 31 32 7 6 5 4 3 2 1

This book is dedicated to Dr. Lynn Cohick, who is both a mentor and a friend. I met Dr. Cohick on my first day as a doctoral candidate at Denver Seminary in 2019 (where she was then serving as provost), at which point she effectively hoisted me onto her petite shoulders and carried me across the graduation line at Houston Theological Seminary in 2026. She exemplifies the beautiful combination of academic brilliance and others-oriented kindness, proving theological acumen is more about loving God and people than it is about accumulating spiritual data.

contents

FOREWORD

In 2016, at the excavation of an Israeli archaeological site called Lachish, scientists recovered a small ivory comb amongst the Canaanite artifacts. It wasn't until 2021 that a research associate at Hebrew University of Jerusalem was examining the comb and decided to take a photo of it with her iPhone. Finding the lighting inadequate and the resulting image unsatisfactory, she moved the artifact into brighter light in order to get a clearer picture.

As she did so, seventeen letters ranging in size from one to three millimeters and carved into the comb itself suddenly became visible. She was looking at humanity's first alphabet. Though for many millennia humans had inscribed their communication using pictographs or symbols, these seventeen letters were from the oldest known alphabet that had been created by the Canaanites and used for hundreds of years before becoming the foundation of the ancient Greek and Latin writing systems.[1] These in turn were the foundation for the language and alphabet in which I am writing this very sentence.

1. Margaret Osborne, "Scientists Translate the Oldest Sentence Written in the First Alphabet," *Smithsonian Magazine*, November 10, 2022, https://www.smithsonianmag.com/smart-news/scientists-translate-the-oldest-sentence-written-in-the-first-alphabet-180981101/.

Though small groups of letters from this alphabet had been found previously, the 2021 discovery was different, as the seventeen letters formed the earliest preserved complete written sentence in human history. This is what it said: "May this tusk root out the lice of the hair and the beard."[2]

That's right. The oldest known preserved sentence was about lice, and it was on an implement designed to get rid of those gross little parasitic bugs that make us itch just thinking about them. As one of the scientists observed, these words are so human. So practical. Now, as then, humans use words to identify and diagnose our afflictions, and we are grateful when we come across words that are prescriptions of remedy.

Though we are born with an ingrained instinct to communicate and connect, words come later for us humans. Language is heard before it is learned, formed, and repeated. Our infant grunts and gurgles become a jumble of consonants and vowels tumbling around drooly mouths. Gradually—at first simply and soon with greater complexity—these sounds form words. We start by repeating them, singing them, and speaking them, and eventually we learn to read and write them.

As we are communicated to in phrases and sentences and stories, we soon learn to speak and write our own phrases, sentences, and stories. We use them to convey our basic needs, to describe our inner and outer worlds, our spiritual and practical delights, our desires and afflictions.

To accurately communicate—and be communicated to—we need the right words.

Just as the words on that ancient ivory comb were obscured and indecipherable until seen in the right light, Lisa Harper has spent her life masterfully using her God-given gift of language to help illuminate the Word for us. She points us always to the God of Scripture and to Christ, the Living Word, who is present throughout it. And it holds a far better message than

2. Osborne, "Oldest Sentence Written."

a Canaanite remedy for lice—the complete redemptive remedy to a much darker malady.

Ultimately, this is why Lisa wrote *Theology for the Rest of Us*. She gives us words that help us describe and diagnose our failures and deceptions, and that illuminate for us the character, attributes, ways, and heart of our Creator Redeemer (one of Lisa's favorite ways of describing God). Her book spells out in metaphorical CAPS the glorious Good News of the gospel.

A. W. Tozer, one of Lisa's "theological boyfriends," writes, "The best book is not one that informs merely, but one that stirs the reader up to inform himself."[3] I believe this brilliantly thoughtful and helpful book and each of the definitions it contains are warm invitations for precisely that and beyond—information unto revelation.

Brooke Ligertwood,
internationally acclaimed worship leader, artist, and Grammy winner

3. A. W. Tozer, *Man: The Dwelling Place of God* (Christian Publications, 1966), 149.

INTRODUCTION

I'll never forget pulling into the driveway of our country cottage for the very first time with my adopted four-year-old daughter, Missy, sitting wide-eyed in her car seat behind me on April 14, 2014. We'd been traveling for almost eighteen hours by that point—from her orphanage in Haiti to the busy airport in Port-au-Prince to the Miami airport, where we waited through long lines in customs and Homeland Security, to the back row of a regional American Airlines plane to the *C* concourse in the Nashville airport, which led to a cheering crew of friends and family near baggage claim, some of whom walked us out to our SUV and waved as we set off on the inaugural forty-five-minute drive home through a spring thunderstorm. Of course, I talked to her softly the whole time, explaining what was going on and assuring her that she was safe. At one point I even pulled off the interstate into the parking lot of a gas station and crawled into the back seat to hold her and assure her that everything was going to be okay. Poor little thing was more overwhelmed and discombobulated than I was.

I hoped she'd begin to relax when we got to our little farmette and she could see the rolling hills and smell the flowers I'd planted especially for her. But as soon as I pulled up the driveway and opened her door, Missy's anxiety increased because my rowdy trio of dogs were jumping on the fence next to the car and barking "WELCOME HOME" in a loud, enthusiastic chorus. Throughout our two-year adoption process, I'd brought items Missy had worn—like a pair of her socks or one of her tiny T-shirts—home from Haiti so my spoiled, squirrel-chasing canines (Cookie, a lab mix, and Dottie and Harley, who were both Jack Russell terriers) could get used to her scent. To say they were more than ready to envelop her with gleeful sniffs and sloppy licks the second I pulled her out of her car seat is putting it mildly!

However, Missy's response to their raucous show of affection was to shriek and wrap her arms tightly around my neck in terror. Their puppy love was completely unrequited because the caretakers at Missy's orphanage had warned the children never to go near dogs because dogs would eat them. And while I don't condone scaring kids, I did notice lots of wild, reportedly rabid dogs every time I visited Haiti. Frankly, some people there don't have enough money to feed their families, so having enough resources to feed and care for a pet is a luxury many can't afford, which is why lots of cats and dogs roam free on the island and can be quite aggressive. Therefore, the caretakers' fearmongering and my little girl's initial distress about animals was understandable.

But Cookie, a gentle mutt I'd rescued from a shelter for animals who'd been abused the same season I started the adoption process with Missy, soon eased my daughter's apprehension. Every night when I let Cookie into the house, she'd carefully ease to within a few feet of wherever Missy was sitting, then roll over onto her back, expose her pink belly, and wag her tail softly from side to side, as if to say, "Come here and pet me, little girl. I promise I won't hurt you." It took a week or so for me to coax Missy into rubbing her belly, but she finally relented and then giggled when Cookie's tongue lolled happily out of her mouth and her tail began thumping faster, due to the long-awaited rub.

Cookie was the first animal Missy ever loved and her best buddy until the day we had to say goodbye. Tears rolled down our vet's face, and I caressed Cookie's noble head in my lap until her eyes closed for good. Missy's bond with her was mostly due to Cookie's nonthreatening demeanor, but her name helped too (volunteers at the shelter named her Cookie because the black spots on her white coat reminded them of cookies-and-cream ice cream) since *cookie* was one of the few English words Missy knew when I brought her home and they were a rare treat in Haiti. I think from the very beginning, she subconsciously associated Cookie's moniker with something sweet and special. She never developed the same close bond with our other dogs. She *tolerated* Dottie and Harley, but she *adored* Cookie. When Missy called her, she even elongated the first syllable and emphasized the second, like "Cuuuhhh-KEY," as if she wanted to hold on to the pleasing sound of her furry friend's name as long as possible. The word itself carried the promise of something good.

The reason I wrote this little layman's dictionary of fifty theological terms is because these words/names—a few of which admittedly sound overtly academic and inscrutable at first—carry the promise of very *good* things about our Savior! We were created by a trinitarian God who wants to be in a real, vibrant, and increasingly intimate relationship with us. You certainly don't have to know—much less know how to pronounce—multisyllabic seminary terms to have faith in Jesus. But if you choose to peruse the following pages, somewhere in your sanctified imagination you might just catch a glimpse of our perfectly holy and transcendent Creator Redeemer rolling over onto His glorious back and beckoning you to scooch closer.

1

Advent

■ **ADVENT:** Comes from the Latin word *adventus,* which means "arrival" or "coming."

In the Christian tradition, *Advent* refers to a celebratory ritual that takes place on the four Sundays leading up to Christmas. It involves the use of an evergreen Advent wreath with four differently colored candles (typically some variation of purple, blue, and pink) in the circle, surrounding one white candle in the middle. The candles are lit one at a time on successive Sundays, symbolizing the hope, love, joy, and peace that accompany the advent/arrival of Jesus Christ. The final white "Christ candle" in the center of the Advent wreath is lit on Christmas Eve or Christmas Day, symbolizing that Jesus Christ—the Light of the World—has come.

Historically, Advent was only observed in liturgical churches such as Catholic, Lutheran, Anglican, and Methodist. However, celebrating Advent has become increasingly common in other Christian denominations and in non/multidenominational worship gatherings. And while the specific word *advent* isn't found in the Bible, there are multiple Old Testament prophecies about the first advent/arrival of the Messiah (Isa. 7:14; 9:2–7; Mic. 5:2; Mal. 3:1–3), as well as multiple New Testament prophecies about the second advent/arrival—the triumphant return—of Jesus Christ (Matt. 24:30, 42–44; Acts 1:11; 1 Cor. 15:51–52; 1 Thess. 4:16–17; Rev. 1:7).

The celebration of Advent dates all the way back to the fourth and fifth centuries AD when it marked the season of preparation for the baptism of new Christians at the January feast of Epiphany. During that ancient season of preparation, Christ followers spent forty days in penance, prayer, and fasting prior to Epiphany. In fact, it wasn't until the Middle Ages that Advent became solely connected with the birth of Jesus. And while joy was certainly one facet of those old Advent celebrations, the season included sobriety as well for our ancestors of the faith because they spent much of those forty days marinating in the harsh reality that our Messiah's incarnation was necessitated by our need for a Savior. That He *had to be born in order to die,* because His blood was the only thing that could atone for our sins. Early practitioners of Advent viewed Christmas through the lens of Good Friday. Their posture was one of humility and hope. Loss and longing. Waiting and wonder. It revealed the juxtapositional reality of our existence between two advents—the first, when the Divine came to earth in a suit of skin as Immanuel, and the second, when King Jesus will return triumphantly to claim us as His bride.

Dietrich Bonhoeffer described the poignant posture of humility and hope, loss and longing, waiting and wonder in this keen literary observation: "The celebration of Advent is possible only to those who are troubled in soul, who know themselves to be poor and imperfect, and who look forward to something greater to come."[1] And my daughter, Missy, modeled Bonhoeffer's description in a way I'll always remember the first Advent season we got to celebrate together, just a few months after I brought her home from Haiti.

It happened in December 2014, when I took her for her first photo session with Santa. (I know some of you probably winced when you read that last bit

1. Timothy George, "Bonhoeffer in Advent," The International Bonhoeffer Society, accessed October 14, 2025, https://bonhoeffersociety.org/bonhoeffer-in-advent/.

because y'all think only pagans and the backslidden let their children take pictures with Santa Claus. However, I'd like to remind you that I didn't get to become Missy's second mama until the year I turned fifty, and after trying to keep a stiff upper lip through dozens of "single and childless" holidays, I'll be darned if I wasn't going to have at least one picture of my precious baby girl with good ole *St. Nick*! Anyway, please keep reading, because I can assure you I did my level best to put the whole nostalgic experience in proper biblical context.) Missy was five years old then, spoke very little English, had never really celebrated Christmas in Haiti, and was thoroughly confused about all the hubbub concerning the pudgy dude in the red velvet suit.

I didn't want to confuse her with sentimentalism, but I also didn't want to snuff out the faint glimmer of innocent anticipation she had regarding her first Christmas. So I did my best to explain that the whole point of Christmas was Jesus's birthday—that it was when we celebrate Him coming to earth and being born as a baby boy in Bethlehem who would grow up to become the Savior of the world and who is now in heaven, sitting at the right hand of our heavenly Father and "interceding"—or talking to God—about us. Then I carefully explained how Santa is sort of like a human cartoon (although his character is based on a historical figure named Saint Nicholas) who helps deliver presents every December, and since he isn't invisible like Jesus, he tends to get a lot of attention even though it isn't *his* birthday. I'm sure you can imagine that by the time I finished my merry monologue Missy's wariness had increased, as was evidenced by her extreme reticence to sit on Santa's lap.

I was finally able to coax her into posing for a picture with him, but she made it clear that she wasn't happy about it. She arched her tiny body away from him, gave him some serious stink eye, and then asked with gruff suspicion, "Do you know Jebus?" I could tell that kind faux Santa was flustered when he cocked his head a smidge and asked gently, "What did you say, honey?" At which point, Missy's eyebrows furrowed, and she repeated the question more emphatically. "DO. YOU. KNOW. JEBUS?" The poor guy glanced over at me with a *Please help me out here, Lady!* expression because she had such a thick Creole accent, he couldn't understand her. So I quickly explained how I'd told her that Santa was simply one of Jesus's friends here on earth who helps with all the birthday festivities. At which point that dear man turned to Missy and exclaimed joyfully, "Ho, ho, ho, I sure do know Jesus, honey . . . He's my very best friend!"

I still find myself smiling when I think about my daughter's innocent boldness with Mr. Claus and her insistency about Jesus. Even at five, Missy knew who the real hero of Christmas was, and her preoccupation with the Prince of Peace is the very essence of Advent. *Immanuel,* which means "God with us," underscores the fact that King Jesus compassionately stooped to become incarnate (Australian theologian John Nolland describes Christ's incarnation as the "divine condescension"[2]). And that—the miraculous *withness of God*—is the invaluable prize of Advent, completely eclipsing the anticipatory joy of trillions upon trillions of miniature chocolates hiding behind petite doorways on holiday-themed calendars!

■ **WHY *ADVENT* MATTERS:** Advent matters because it gives us a marked time in our calendars when we're encouraged to ponder the profound significance of the incarnation—the "withness" of God through Immanuel. And when Christ followers reflect on Jesus's first advent, it should fertilize our hope and anticipation regarding the second advent, when our Savior will return victoriously to claim us as His bride! Therefore, not only does Advent allow us a respite from the chaotic commercialism that can mute the true miracle of Christmas, it also provides an annual spiritual reset.

---

2. John Nolland, *Word Biblical Commentary: Luke 1–9:20* (Word Books, 1989), 111.

2

Anthropomorphism

■ **ANTHROPOMORPHISM:** "The attribution of human characteristics or behavior to a god, animal, or object."[1]

A friend of mine told me a story several years ago that I thought was priceless. It was about a bright little boy in a kindergarten Sunday school class. It was the Sunday before Easter, and the Sunday school teacher wanted to remind the children what Easter was all about. So she started by asking the class a question that would help them understand that many of the traditional holidays we celebrate center around Jesus.

"Who can tell me the meaning of Christmas?" she asked.

One of the six-year-old boys raised his hand and said, "It's when Jesus became incarnate, and all the angels sang, and the shepherds worshiped, and the wise men came."

"That was an excellent answer, Billy," the teacher said, thinking, *Wow, his parents must be teachers or something*. Then she asked, "Now, who can tell us the meaning of today, Palm Sunday?"

1. *Webster's Encyclopedic Unabridged Dictionary of the English Language*, new deluxe ed. (Thunder Bay, 2001), under "anthropomorphism."

The same little boy raised his hand and answered, "It's when Jesus entered Jerusalem as the Messiah, and all the people laid down palm branches, and it was the beginning of the last week of His life."

The teacher grinned at Billy's enthusiastic response and continued her line of questioning. "Can anyone else explain what happened on Good Friday?"

The rest of the little boys and girls were quiet and wide-eyed, unsure of the answer. After waiting for someone else to speak up, the teacher nodded at young Einstein, and he answered again: "That's when Jesus was crucified on a cross for our sins, and the temple curtain was torn in two, and He gave up His spirit to the Father."

Impressed and bemused, the teacher smiled at Billy and said, "Well, honey, why don't you go ahead and explain Easter?"

Billy straightened his shoulders, cleared his throat, and proudly proclaimed, "That's when Jesus came out of the tomb, but then He saw His shadow, so He went back in for another three weeks!"

Although most of us probably wouldn't confuse the resurrection of God Incarnate with Groundhog Day, we do get our wires crossed when it comes to understanding everything about our Creator Redeemer! And quite frankly, it's impossible to discern *everything* about Him because God can't be distilled into someone who *can* be perfectly understood by created beings like us. Simply put, His infinite majesty is more than our finite minds can comprehend.

Unfortunately, we tend to forget that and compensate by creating mental caricatures of God like some cartoon deity. Ancient church father Blaise Pascal, who was also a mathematician, philosopher, and certified brainiac, observed wisely, "God made man in his own image and man returned the compliment."[2] Martin Luther made a similar observation when he chastised Erasmus with

2. Quoted in Brennan Manning, *Abba's Child: The Cry of the Heart for Intimate Belonging* (NavPress, 1994), 15.

this stinging rebuke: "Your thoughts of God are all too human."[3] And modern theologian Gerald Bray echoed their sentiments in his book *The Doctrine of God* when he wrote, "An overemphasis on knowing God in personal relationship can so easily lead to a semi-conscious denigration of his divinity, and a loss of a sense of his glorious power and majesty."[4]

Now, before your neck gets all splotchy and you succumb to shame because you've been guilty of "semi-conscious denigration of his divinity" by using anthropomorphisms to understand or talk about God, let me be the first one to put my hand up. More importantly, let me encourage you with the fact that the Bible actually uses anthropomorphic terminology—like when David wrote,

> When I consider your heavens,
> *the work of your fingers,*
> the moon and the stars,
> which you have set in place,
> what is mankind that you are mindful of them,
> human beings that you care for them? (Ps. 8:3–4)

Furthermore, during Jesus's incarnate ministry here on earth, He *did* have human form and attributes, so a few anthropomorphisms here and there are wholly appropriate when it comes to understanding God and His Word. They're just kind of like using dill in a recipe—a little bit goes a long way!

A simple and effective way I've found to remember the meaning—and potential misuse—of anthropomorphisms is visualizing the first three letters, *ant,* because the visual image of that wee insect helps me to be more mindful about the internal and external language I wrap around my understanding of God, lest I make Him way too small in my mind and conversations.

3. Quoted in Arthur W. Pink, *The Attributes of God* (Baker Books, 1975), 28.
4. Gerald Bray, *The Doctrine of God,* Contours of Christian Theology (IVP Academic, 1993), 106.

- **WHY *ANTHROPOMORPHISM* MATTERS:** Anthropomorphism matters because, in the context of Christianity, it's a form of analogy that helps humans better understand and relate to divine realities. However, it's also important for Christ followers to recognize that anthropomorphisms can overly simplify or contextualize God in a way that leads us away from what He reveals about Himself through Holy Writ and Holy Spirit.

3

Apocalypse

APOCALYPSE: Derived from the Greek word *apokalupsis,* which means to "uncover" or "reveal."[1] The related descriptive term *apocalyptic* refers to a genre of revelatory literature that depicts cosmic events, including the final destruction of the world, as described in the biblical books of Daniel and Revelation. Apocalyptic writing typically features characters moving between heaven, earth, and hell and depicts cosmic conflicts involving angels and human armies against divine powers.[2] Because *apocalypse* is typically used in relation to eschatology (the study of the "last days / end times"), the phrase *the apocalypse* is also used to describe the cataclysmic end of the world as we know it, which is prophesied in Daniel 10–12, Mark 13, 2 Peter 3, and throughout the book of Revelation.

When I was in high school, my boyfriend and I—who thought we were madly in love and going to get married after college—got caught "parking" by two policemen who went to great lengths to scare the amorous out of us. They

1. Catherine Soanes and Angus Stevenson, eds., *Concise Oxford English Dictionary,* 11th ed. (Oxford University Press, 2004), under "apocalypse."

2. George Thomas Kurian and James D. Smith III, eds., *The Encyclopedia of Christian Literature,* vol. 1, *Genres and Types/Biographies A–G* (Scarecrow Press, 2010), under "apocalyptic literature."

turned on their sirens and blue lights, approached our car with a high-powered flashlight, then made us roll down the fogged-up windows and asked for both of our driver's licenses. After studying them for several terrifying minutes, they handed them back to us with a look of stern disapproval, which was followed by a lecture about the possible dangers of our extracurricular activity.

For those of you who are under the age of forty, *parking* is a term we older folks used to describe making out in a stationary automobile. And for those of you who may be wondering how in the world I can remember something that took place over forty years ago with such vivid detail—my clear recall is because it happened twice. A week or so after having the wits scared out of us for kissing in a parked car, the same officers busted us for stationary smooching *again*! Which not only made my face turn beet red, it made my heart almost beat out of my chest because those lawmen not only threatened to call our parents, they threatened *to take us to jail*! Of course, they were probably just bemused and trying to frighten us into more chaste behavior because our stammering "Yes, sir" and "No, sir" replies to their inquiries, coupled with our clean-cut appearances, didn't exactly scream "dangerous juvenile delinquents." But we were only seventeen years old at the time, which meant our frontal lobes weren't fully developed, so I was seized with the panicky thought, *This is going to be like one of those* Charlie's Angels *episodes, where I'm sent to a women's prison in the boonies and forced to work on a chain gang while wearing an ill-fitting denim jumpsuit.*

Unfortunately, some folks have a similar reaction when they hear the word *apocalypse*. Well, maybe not the part about a prison jumpsuit, but *apocalypse* tends to ping a primal fear too. The word itself sounds ominous, as if it represents a sharp left turn into something terrible. Something that threatens our very existence as human beings. Finding out that its definition is simply to "uncover" or "reveal" causes an internal sort of head tilt, doesn't it? Like, *Wow, I thought it'd be much more terrifying than that.* If you're a Christ follower, you can stop clenching and wincing when you hear the word *apocalypse* or find out your pastor is doing a series on Revelation because the monstrous, catastrophic, warring imagery "revealed" in those passages is in reference to the *foes* of God, and Scripture makes it clear that if you've put your hope in Jesus, you're in His *family*. In other words, the battle for you has already been won. Consider the following passage:

> But in those days, following that distress,
>
> > *"the sun will be darkened,*
> > *and the moon will not give its light;*
> > *the stars will fall from the sky,*
> > *and the heavenly bodies will be shaken."* (Mark 13:24–25)

At first this sounds like the scriptural version of that scary, two-note musical motif from the movie *Jaws*: *dun-dun . . . dun-dun . . . dun-dun-dun-dun-dun-dun*. Goodness gracious, if someone played those same repetitive, low-pitched E and F notes while I was waiting for the boat to come around and pick me up after a wakesurfing fall in the lake here in Tennessee—here we have bluegill and bass and catfish but *no* sharks—I'd probably pull a Pete and try to walk on top of the water to get to the boat! But now consider that passage in conjunction with Matthew's narrative of Jesus's crucifixion:

> *From noon until three in the afternoon darkness came over all the land.*
>
> About three in the afternoon Jesus cried out in a loud voice, "Eli, Eli, lema sabachthani?" (which means "My God, my God, why have you forsaken me?").
>
> When some of those standing there heard this, they said, "He's calling Elijah."
>
> Immediately one of them ran and got a sponge. He filled it with wine vinegar, put it on a staff, and offered it to Jesus to drink. The rest said, "Now leave him alone. Let's see if Elijah comes to save him."
>
> And when Jesus had cried out again in a loud voice, he gave up his spirit.

> At that moment the curtain of the temple was torn in two from top to bottom. *The earth shook, the rocks split* and the tombs broke open. The bodies of many holy people who had died were raised to life. They came out of the tombs after Jesus' resurrection and went into the holy city and appeared to many people.
>
> When the centurion and those with him who were guarding Jesus *saw the earthquake* and all that had happened, they were terrified, and exclaimed, "Surely he was the Son of God!" (Matt. 27:45–54)

Distress, darkness, rocks splitting, the earth quaking . . . sounds familiar, doesn't it? The bottom line is that the worst of judgment has already happened, and Jesus took the brunt of it on the cross! He received the wrath of God for sinners—He sufficiently dealt with the darkness that came when God turned His face away from our iniquity. Therefore, the scary stuff depicted in prophetic, apocalyptic imagery doesn't represent what's around the corner for those who've put their hope in the Son of God; that dreadful imagery is for those who haven't.

Despite my brief proclivity for parking in high school, which led to those oh-so-embarrassing confrontations with the law, I've only had to go to court one time in my life for a speeding ticket. Therefore, I don't know what it feels like to stand at the defense table before a judge who's about to give me the death penalty. And the Bible makes it clear that's the consequence for sin, for how we humans have all rebelled against a Holy God (see Rom. 3:23). However, when we place the apocalyptic warnings in Daniel, Mark, and Revelation under the umbrella of the divine grace poured out for us through the life, death, and resurrection of Jesus Christ, it becomes clear that the Great Judge of the universe set down His gavel, took off His robe, stepped down from His seat of honor, approached the proven guilty defendant of humanity, enveloped us in a compassionate embrace, then nudged us to the side and received the full punishment of death that we deserve.

Jesus didn't just pardon our sins—*He took our place!*

- **WHY *APOCALYPSE* MATTERS:** Apocalyptic prophecies and imagery illustrate that life as we understand it here on earth *will come to an end*. There will come a point when those who haven't yet put their hope in the unconditional love of Jesus Christ will no longer have the chance to. The wrath depicted in apocalyptic writings shouldn't *scare* Christ followers because Jesus has already received the punishment we deserve. But they can compel us to *share* the saving grace of the gospel with as many people as we can, as often as we can.

4

Apophatic Theology

APOPHATIC THEOLOGY: *Apophasis* comes from the Greek root words *apo,* which means "away from," and *phasis,* which means "statement." Therefore, apophatic theology is based on the premise that human reasoning and language are too limited to fully comprehend and describe an infinite God.[1]

It's basically a spirituality of negation. It's a way of saying, "God is so much more than all of this!" Because the minute we proclaim, "God is holy," we effectively negate His holiness with an inadequate human adjective. This way of thinking about God is particularly prominent in Eastern Orthodox Christianity, where conversations about God are often framed by what He is *not,* as opposed to what He *is.*[2] And while this type of "negative spirituality" can appear to diminish personal, relational experience with God, practitioners insist it helps them become more aware of God's transcendence and enjoy a genuine union with Him through prayer.[3]

1. Eve Tibbs, *A Basic Guide to Eastern Orthodox Theology: Introducing Beliefs and Practices* (Baker Academic, 2021), 180.
2. F. L. Cross and Elizabeth A. Livingstone, eds., *The Oxford Dictionary of the Christian Church* (Oxford University Press, 2005), under "apophatic theology."
3. B. Nassif, "Apophatic Theology," in *New Dictionary of Theology: Historical and Systematic,* ed. Martin Davie et al. (InterVarsity Press, 2016), 52.

Apophatic theology—or apophatic spirituality—is often contrasted with kataphatic (or affirmative) theology/spirituality, which makes positive statements about God's attributes and presumes that humans can *know* Him, at least in part. Conversely, apophatic theology is a means to affirm God's transcendence and the supernatural mystery of our Creator Redeemer, basically His "unknowability." It's what David was overwhelmed by in Psalm 8:

> LORD, our LORD,
> how majestic is your name in all the earth!
>
> You have set your glory
> in the heavens.
> Through the praise of children and infants
> you have established a stronghold against your enemies,
> to silence the foe and the avenger.
> *When I consider your heavens,*
> *the work of your fingers,*
> *the moon and the stars,*
> *which you have set in place,*
> *what is mankind that you are mindful of them,*
> *human beings that you care for them?* (vv. 1–4)

And while there are obvious dangers to thinking about God in wholly unknowable terms—*apophatic* is related to the pejorative terms *apostasy* and *agnostic*—there are some benefits to recognizing that the God of creation cannot be completely distilled into something our dinky human minds can perfectly wrap themselves around.

For instance, our early church leaders employed apophatic theology when they shaped the doctrinal language of Christianity through the ecumenical councils (AD 325–787). The creeds (such as the Nicene Creed and the Apostles' Creed), which establish the scaffolding and boundaries of our belief system, don't provide simplistic answers or fully resolve every question about the

Christian faith. They are not ends in themselves. Instead, our "credos of faith" were initially written to protect the Christian church from heresies that were attempting to do that very thing—to put God in a box, if you will.

Frankly, in the 1,700 years that have passed since Christian orthodoxy began to be formally shaped at the Council of Nicaea, countless more misunderstandings about God have arisen. Heresies within our belief system are like the "whack-a-mole" arcade game—just about the time we slam one stinker back into the "biblically indefensible" hole where it belongs, another one pops up! The bottom line is our understanding about God will *always* be limited here on earth. Which means some facets of our faith will *always* be challenged by well-intentioned and not-so-well-intentioned people. And some of the questions that both Christians and non-Christians pose about God won't be fully answered until we see Him face-to-face in Glory, about which David prophetically enthused,

> As for me, I will be vindicated and will see your face;
> when I awake, *I will be satisfied with seeing your likeness.*
> (Ps. 17:15)

In other words, even if we still can't fully comprehend everything about our trinitarian God when we're united with Him in heaven, the mysteries about Him won't cramp our brains anymore. Because the Hebrew phrase *will be satisfied* that David used in Psalm 17:15 means that all our expectations will be met. No more feeling confused about multisyllabic theological terms, no more wondering if the burning question we have about God will sound dumb if we pose it to our small group, and no more thinking, *I have no earthly idea why our pastor gets so excited about stuff like ancient Greek verb tenses—I'm not an old Greek person, and I just wish he'd tell another funny story*. Instead, we'll be able to peacefully exhale into the glorious vastness of our Creator Redeemer.

In the meantime, I think it behooves us to do some intentional exhaling into His glorious vastness in the here and now. I became Missy's second mama relatively late in life. I was forty-six years old when dear Marie—whom I *can't wait* to meet in heaven—gave birth to Missy; forty-eight years old when Marie died, after which, by God's grace, I got woven into Missy's story; and fifty years old when I got to bring her home through the miracle of adoption. To say she brought a fresh infusion of wonder and awe into my middle-aged life is putting it mildly! Obviously, a four-year-old who couldn't yet speak English wasn't able to appreciate it when I tried to explain God to her with words, so we got into the habit of going outside at night, lying in the grass, and looking up at the stars. We live on top of a steep hill in a rural area, so we don't have much light pollution, and we have an unobscured view of the sky. On a clear night there are *so many* stars to ponder, I think one star-appreciation session could remedy anyone's awe-deprivation!

Even though she's a teenager now, Missy still grass-gazes on a regular basis with me at night. And most of the time, we just lie there side by side without saying much. We let our minds get quiet and our hearts gape over the unfathomable mystery of an eternal God who set billions of stars in the sky yet also knows the exact number of chemically dependent (mine) and gorgeously curly (hers) hairs on our heads, right here in the boonies of Middle Tennessee. He is transcendent *and* imminent. Cosmically authoritative *and* relationally accessible. Like most everything else in life, apophatic spirituality is best enjoyed in moderation. But it should be *enjoyed.*

■ **WHY *APOPHATIC THEOLOGY* MATTERS:** Gaping at the unfathomable mystery of an eternal God helps our hearts and minds remember that He is the Creator and we are His created. God the Father, God the Son, God the Spirit is not our peer or copilot; He is the Creator, Sustainer, and Redeemer of the universe. The wonder that results from a healthy measure of apophatic theology can fertilize both our humility and our gratitude that the only true God—who breathed myriads of galaxies into existence—loves mere humans like us.

5

Arianism

ARIANISM: One of the most powerful and tenacious heresies in the history of Christianity. It was first preached in the fourth century by a prominent priest named Arius, who insisted that Jesus the Son of God was of a lesser nature than God the Father.

Have you ever heard someone use the expression "Not one iota" to emphasize the lack of something? For instance, if a waiter at a Tex-Mex restaurant asked whether it mattered if they served me yellow or blue corn tortilla chips with queso, I might reply, "Not one iota . . . as long as you bring an entire basketful!" The reason "one iota" is associated with nothing—or next to nothing—is because *iota* is the smallest letter in the Greek alphabet. But oddly enough, the wee iota made a massive difference in Christian doctrine!

Here's how it all began: Arius's basic argument was that since Jesus Christ was the *son* of God, He couldn't possibly be equal with God because sons are born/created (he got pretty hung up on the word *begotten* from John 3:16). Therefore, Arius deduced that, unlike God the Father, Jesus couldn't have existed eternally. In other words, Jesus's deity was "derived." And while He has a unique and exceptional creaturely status—having been created before all other things—the fact that Jesus was born/created like all other creatures made Him less "divine" than God the Father. He could be the "Son of God," but He couldn't be "God the Son" too.

Arius and his followers even had a slogan for their heretical belief regarding the "created" and therefore lesser nature of Jesus: *There was a time when he was not.* That rallying cry spread throughout the church in Africa, forcing the bishop of Alexandria to excommunicate Arius in AD 318. He then relocated to Israel, where his views gained traction and soon spread throughout civilization, creating schisms among Christian leaders and their respective churches.

This disunity is what ultimately led to the Council of Nicaea, which was the first formal gathering of Christian leaders in AD 325—called for and paid for by Emperor Constantine, the most powerful man in the world at that time and a recent convert to Christianity. This ancient conference of Christian leaders included about three hundred bishops representing churches from across the Roman Empire, including Greece, the Middle East, Africa, Italy, and Spain. They met, ate, argued, and prayed together for two months to create a statement of faith that would unify the global Christian church. It became known as the Nicene Creed.

The most important doctrine formalized in the Nicene Creed is the doctrine of the Trinity—God the Father, God the Son, and God the Spirit. And the Greek term those bishops in Nicaea used to describe the Trinity was *homoousios,* which comes from the root words *homo,* meaning "same," and *ousia,* meaning "substance." It unequivocally affirms that Jesus Christ, the Son of God, is of the *exact same substance* as God the Father; therefore, He *is* fully divine and God the Son.

All but three of the three hundred or so bishops who attended the Council of Nicaea (including Saint Nicholas of Myra, who later became the "man behind the myth" of Santa Claus![1]) signed the Nicene Creed. The proverbial

1. Bryan M. Litfin, *The Story of the Trinity: Controversy, Crisis, and the Creation of the Nicene Creed* (Baker Books, 2025), 125.

flies in the ointment of Christian unity were, of course, Arius along with two other bishops he'd hoodwinked with his heretical views. That trio of stumbling saints was kicked out of the council for stubbornly insisting on the "lesser than" nature of Jesus. However, not unlike the mint that runs rampant in my garden, the roots of Arianism were hard to kill, and a theological movement that challenged the orthodox view of the Trinity persisted for centuries after the Council of Nicaea. The Greek term they used to describe the Trinity wasn't *homoousios*—"same substance"—instead, it was *homoiousios*, which comes from the root words *homoios*, meaning "like," and *ousia*, meaning "substance." The only difference between those fancy theological words is an itsy-bitsy *i*, but that one iota makes all the difference!

- **WHY *ARIANISM* MATTERS:** Understanding a pervasive heresy like Arianism matters because it helps Christ followers recognize and refute doctrinal beliefs that are counterfeit to biblical Christianity.

6

Atonement

ATONEMENT: In Christian thought, the act by which God and humans are brought together in a personal relationship.

The term is derived from Anglo-Saxon words meaning "making at one," hence "at-one-ment." It presupposes a separation or alienation that needs to be overcome if human beings are to know God and have fellowship with Him. As a term expressing relationship, *atonement* is tied closely to such terms as *reconciliation* and *forgiveness*.[1]

My cultural roots are sunk in the Deep South of the United States, which means—besides twanging when I talk and stubbornly holding on to the notion that "the higher the hair, the closer to God"—I come from a lineage of women who have strong opinions about the correct ingredients to put in chicken salad. And none of the women in my family agree on what they are! My mom is resolute about including Hellmann's mayonnaise, freshly shelled pecans, and halved red grapes, while one of my aunts (all of whom shall remain nameless lest I get stink-eyed at our next family reunion) prefers walnuts instead

1. Robert W. Lyon and Peter Toon, "Atonement," in *Baker Encyclopedia of the Bible*, vol. 1 (Baker Book House, 1988), 231.

of pecans, and still another liberally decorates hers with paprika because it reminds her of the chicken salad she ordered once at a nice restaurant. But at the end of the day, all of their recipes depend on one key, absolutely *necessary*, ingredient: shredded chicken.

There have probably been as many theories on atonement throughout the history of the Christian church and across the beautiful breadth of our denominations (according to recent research, there are currently around forty-one thousand distinct denominations in Christianity[2]) as there are chicken salad recipes in the American South. However, the one key, absolutely *necessary*, ingredient of atonement is the sinless life, sacrificial death, and subsequent resurrection of Jesus Christ!

Three of the most common "recipes" regarding atonement are as follows:

1. **Ransom Theory:** This theory suggests Jesus's death was a ransom paid, often to Satan, to liberate humanity from the bondage of sin and death.
2. **Satisfaction Theory:** This theory posits that Jesus's death satisfied the honor or justice of God, offering a perfect sacrifice to compensate for the offense of human sin.
3. **Penal Substitution Theory:** A development of the Satisfaction Theory, this emphasizes that Jesus endured the punishment (penalty) for human sin in our place (substitution), thereby satisfying God's wrath and allowing for forgiveness.

Yes, there are a few differing, unnecessary "ingredients" in these different vantage points of atonement, but the biblical Maypole they all rally around comes from the mouth of our Messiah Himself: "I am the way and the truth and the life. No one comes to the Father except through me" (John 14:6).

2. Dr. Kathleen Mulhern, class lecture notes, Biblical and Historical Foundations of Spiritual Formation, Denver Seminary, July 2021.

Every now and then, when I can't see around the corner of my circumstances, or when I feel alone or misunderstood or just overwhelmed by the dailiness of life, I forget the miracle of getting to experience "at-one-ment" with the Creator of the universe because of the amazing grace of Jesus Christ. Instead, I daydream about a fairy-tale kind of life. One in which all my difficulties and concerns would magically disappear. One in which I'd have a godly husband who dealt with the dead raccoons in the attic (I just *can't*) and helped Missy with her math homework (I just *can't*) and cooked delicious, healthy, low-carb meals every night (I just *can't*). One in which all my friends would truly enjoy listening to long-winded stories and would have more cellulite than me. Honestly, sometimes I wish being a Christian was congruent with an easier, more downhill than uphill existence.

But eventually Holy Spirit will pull me out of my mental ditch and remind me that a Messiah who only served to grant our wishes would be akin to an overindulgent mother who lets her child eat all the candy he wants and stay up as late as he likes and never makes him accept responsibility or obey authority. Pretty soon she's got a middle-aged man with no job, no friends, and no respect for her still living in his boyhood room, demanding Twinkies for lunch.

Jesus didn't die to make us happy. He's not some cartoonish character flitting around in a sparkly outfit and waving a magic wand. He's the sovereign Son of the Most High God. He willingly set down His scepter in glory . . . He shrugged into a suit of skin . . . He lived a perfect, sinless life . . . He submitted to a cruel and humiliating death on a Roman cross . . . He received the wrath of God that we deserved for our depravity . . . He died a bodily death . . . He was buried in a borrowed tomb . . . and He rose again three days later. Now our merciful Savior is sitting at the right hand of God the Father, interceding for us—talking to the CREATOR OF THE UNIVERSE in favorable terms *about prone-to-wander stinkers like us*. They might be going over blueprints of the mansions They've designed for us to enjoy when we're reunited with Them in heaven, where we'll get to gather around a massive banquet table and eat as much and whatever kind of chicken salad we want! Atonement reveals that the dreams Jesus fulfilled for us are infinitely grander than the confines of our dinky minds. If that doesn't get your heart to gaping, then you probably need an EKG.

- **WHY *ATONEMENT* MATTERS:** Atonement matters because it is the hub of our theological wheel as Christians! It connects the dots from sin to salvation. It's the red thread of redemption that leads us through the horrible maze of the Fall all the way to our restoration through faith in Jesus.

7

Bible Translatory Variance

- **BIBLE TRANSLATORY VARIANCE:** The variance in Bible translations arises from several factors, including the absence of original manuscripts, the need for translations into different languages, and the inherent challenges of translating between languages with different structures and nuances.[1] Translators face textual, lexical, literary, and grammatical problems, leading to variations in renderings. Modern translations also differ due to ongoing changes in the English language, varying target audiences, and different choices in underlying Hebrew and Greek texts.[2] Despite these variances, translators generally aim to faithfully reproduce the original text while balancing accuracy and readability.[3]

The original human "authors" of the Bible (they inscribed the words God breathed, so technically our Creator Redeemer is the only *Author* of Scripture!) expressed themselves in three ancient languages—Hebrew, Aramaic, and Greek—none of which are read or spoken by very many modern readers. Therefore, the Bibles

1. Paul W. Downey, "What the Preservation Issue Has Taught Us," in *God's Word in Our Hands: The Bible Preserved for Us*, ed. James B. Williams and Randolph Shaylor (Ambassador Emerald International, 2003), 382.

2. Bruce Manning Metzger, *The Bible in Translation: Ancient and English Versions* (Baker Academic, 2001), 186.

3. Downey, "The Preservation Issue," 382.

we hold dear in modernity are almost all *translations* of the original recorded texts. And let me tell you, there are *a lot* of translations to choose from, and in my experience the issue of people's Bible preference is as emotionally charged as whether they think the toilet paper should roll over or under!

I grew up believing the King James Version of the Bible was the only *real* Bible because my precious Bible banger of a mama said so! She taught us that it was fine to flip through a New International Version or a Living Bible, but when it came to serious study, we could only trust the King James Version because it was *God's favorite Bible*. Mom thought all other translations were inferior scratch-and-dent substitutions. Kind of like the smooshed-up cauliflower that healthy-eating influencers insist tastes just like creamy mashed potatoes with butter (*fat* chance).

After I first learned in seminary that God didn't actually speak Shakespearean English and all those *thee*s and *thou*s were simply the work of ancient translators, I was hesitant to share the news with Mom because I thought she might blow a gasket. She almost took to the bed when I explained how the original King James Version has *more* translatory errors than other translations. This is because the King James Version was the first universally accepted English translation from the Latin Vulgate (which was the first translation from the original Hebrew, Greek, and Aramaic biblical texts compiled mostly by Saint Jerome between AD 382 and 405, as commissioned by Pope Damasus I), and they didn't have computers with sophisticated linguistics programs when it was translated in the 1500s.

Enter a swashbuckling protagonist named William Tyndale, who translated the huge majority of the King James Version of Scripture because he believed regular folks like us should be able to engage with God's living words. Tyndale was an Oxford-educated theologian who later studied at Cambridge, and as he perused the Bible in the original Greek, Hebrew, and Aramaic texts, the idea of translating those words into English began. Although his first English translation of the New Testament was refused permission by a Catholic bishop, Tyndale fled to Germany and printed it anyway. Then—like a top-secret superspy empowered by the Holy Spirit—he smuggled his translation back into England, where it was banned again and often burned in public by priests and politicians. Neither the religious powers that existed in the sixteenth century nor King Henry VIII wanted "normal people" to have access to the Holy Scriptures because if they found out about the unconditional love and liberty God actually promises in those pages, they wouldn't be as easy to manipulate, and unscrupulous yahoos masquerading as church and political leaders wouldn't be able to misuse God's Word to line their own pockets and protect their own power.

Tyndale defied the pope and the Church of England by continuing his translatory work despite the fact that it put his life at risk. He even endured a harrowing shipwreck in 1529 in which all his previous work was destroyed. And yet he pressed on. Five years later, he published revised versions of the New Testament and the book of Genesis and moved to Belgium, where he was ultimately betrayed by someone who posed as a friend and subsequently arrested because his mission to bring God's Word to the masses was perceived as a threat to the money and power of a small minority.

Tyndale spent the last year and a half of his life imprisoned in a dungeon in Brussels. But even that dark, dank place didn't dampen his evangelistic zeal because moments before being strangled and burned at the stake in 1536, that brave martyr prayed out loud, "Lord, open the king of England's eyes."[4] And his prayers were answered because, largely due to public outcry, in 1539 King Henry VIII allowed the Bible in every parish church in England.

Seventy-five years later, King James I came into power and attempted to unify Christians in England by combining the three main English Bibles that were by then in use: the Bishops' Bible (Church of England), the Geneva Bible (Protestants), and the Rheims New Testament (Roman Catholic Church). The resulting "combined" translation was first published in the early 1600s and had the king's name plastered on the cover—the King James Version—to reinforce his image as a political and spiritual leader. If the KJV is your preferred

4. dc Talk and The Voice of the Martyrs, *Jesus Freaks: Stories of Those Who Stood for Jesus, the Ultimate Jesus Freaks* (Asbury Publishing, 1999), 212.

translation of God's Word, you might want to put a piece of duct tape over the royal moniker because it's not *his* Bible! Dr. Timothy George, former dean of Samford University's Beeson Divinity School, underscores the real hero of the easy access we can now enjoy when it comes to God's Word: "The fact that you can hold in your hand and read the Holy Scripture is because of people like William Tyndale who knew that the purity of heart is to will one thing."[5]

It's all I can do not to roll my eyes when I hear people put "boring" and "Bible" in the same sentence, because there's as much drama connected to how our Bible came to be as there is in Tom Cruise's Mission Impossible franchise! Furthermore, according to the American Bible Society, there are now about nine hundred different English translations to choose from. That being said, it can be overwhelming to pick the "right" version(s), so it helps to be acquainted with the three primary styles, or schools of thought, when it comes to Bible translation:

1. **Formal Equivalence**—a word-for-word translation: The idea behind *formal equivalence* is to translate the text as closely as possible to the original, which typically means using the same word order as the original language as well. Examples of formal equivalence in translations would be the New American Standard Bible and the English Standard Version. These literal translations are great for Bible study because of their "as close as we can get to the original language" format. The slight downside of a formal-equivalent translation is that the wording tends to sound a bit formal or clunky.
2. **Dynamic Equivalence** (aka functional equivalence)—a phrase-for-phrase or thought-for-thought translation: The purpose behind *dynamic equivalence* is to render the text in a more relatable format while still faithfully communicating the original writer's intent.

5. Quoted in Mary Wimberley, "Tyndale's Will to 'One Thing' Resulted in English Bible," Samford University, October 30, 2009, https://www.samford.edu/news/2009/Tyndales-Will-to-One-Thing-Resulted-in-English-Bible.

These translations are less concerned with the grammatical form of the original language than they are with the meaning of the original language. Therefore, a dynamic-equivalence translation, like the New International Version or the New Living Translation, tends to be more reader friendly and easier to understand than a formal-equivalence translation. The slight downside of a dynamic-equivalence translation is that there's more room for interpretive bias.

3. **Paraphrase:** Paraphrase Bibles are similar to dynamic-equivalence translations, but they take even more liberties with the original text, use more-simplified phrases, and include more of the translator's perspective on particular passages in order to accommodate a specific audience or reading level. Examples of this kind of translation would be *The Message* or some children's Bibles. Paraphrases are the easiest Bibles to understand, so they're good choices for new believers or children. However, the slight downside of a paraphrase is that they're not nearly as close to the original Hebrew, Greek, and Aramaic texts, and some paraphrase editions leave out certain portions of Scripture, so they're technically incomplete translations.

- **WHY *BIBLE TRANSLATORY VARIANCE* MATTERS:** While there are some disagreements among scholars with regard to Bible translation, most of them are relatively minor and don't challenge the foundational walls of Christian orthodoxy. And the benefit to Bible readers is that having choices regarding our preferred Bible translation(s) means more accessibility to and clarity of God's inscripturated revelation. So I'd encourage you to pick several different versions of actual print Bibles and download a couple of Bible apps that are loaded with all kinds of translations, then dive deep into this incredibly redemptive, God-breathed love story!

8

Christoformity

CHRISTOFORMITY: Being conformed to the principles and disposition of Jesus Christ.[1]

Christoformity, which is basically the process of becoming like Jesus, is related to another, probably more familiar theological term, *sanctification*. The reason I prefer the term *Christoformity* is because the operative root word is *Christ*, and that helps me remember that being conformed to the principles and disposition of Jesus is less about me and more about Him. In other words, living an increasingly Jesus-shaped life is less about the embodiment of biblical ethics and much more so about our relational proximity with Jesus, which leads to us being overwhelmed by His goodness. To become more like Jesus necessitates nearness *to Him* and appreciation *for Him*.

Martyn Lloyd-Jones, a medical doctor and theologian who helped lead the British evangelical movement in the twentieth century and who was the minister of Westminster Chapel in London for thirty years, framed it like this: "The ultimate test of our spirituality is the measure of our amazement at the

1. Scot McKnight, *Pastor Paul: Nurturing a Culture of Christoformity in the Church* (Brazos Press, 2019), 4.

grace of God."[2] And renowned Scottish theologian Sinclair Ferguson made this similar observation linking gratitude and Christoformity: "Being amazed by God's grace is a sign of spiritual vitality. It is a litmus test of how firm and real is our grasp of the Christian gospel and how close is our walk with Jesus Christ."[3]

But surely the most credible proof that being shaped like Jesus is rooted in awed gratitude is evidenced in the life of Peter, the disciple God chose as scaffolding on which to build the early church:

> When Jesus came to the region of Caesarea Philippi, he asked his disciples, "Who do people say the Son of Man is?"
>
> They replied, "Some say John the Baptist; others say Elijah; and still others, Jeremiah or one of the prophets."
>
> "But what about you?" he asked. "Who do you say I am?"
>
> Simon Peter answered, "You are the Messiah, the Son of the living God."
>
> Jesus replied, "Blessed are you, Simon son of Jonah, for this was not revealed to you by flesh and blood, but by my Father in heaven. And I tell you that you are Peter, and on this rock I will build my church, and the gates of Hades will not overcome it." (Matt. 16:13–18)

Over the course of his ministry, Peter matured into such a godly man that his mere shadow had a miraculous healing effect on sick people:

> The apostles performed many signs and wonders among the people. And all the believers used to meet together in Solomon's Colonnade. No one else dared join them, even though they were highly regarded by the people. Nevertheless, more and more men and women believed in the Lord and were added to their number. As a result, people brought the sick into the streets and laid them on beds and mats so that at least Peter's shadow might fall on some of them as he passed by. (Acts 5:12–15)

2. Martyn Lloyd-Jones, *Romans 11: To God's Glory* (Banner of Truth, 1998), 241.
3. Sinclair B. Ferguson, *By Grace Alone: How the Grace of God Amazes Me* (Ligonier Ministries, 2010), xiv.

Ultimately, Peter's Christoformity became *cruciform* (shaped like a cross). History tells us he was martyred on a cross because of his unwavering faith in Jesus—albeit upside down because he didn't consider himself worthy enough to die in the same posture as the Messiah. When it comes to being Christlike, Peter fits the bill.

But we mustn't forget the Benedict Arnold chapter in his story, the fact that he vehemently and vulgarly threw his Messiah and best friend under the bus at Jesus's most desperate moment of need during His incarnate ministry:

> Then seizing him, they led him away and took him into the house of the high priest. Peter followed at a distance. And when some there had kindled a fire in the middle of the courtyard and had sat down together, Peter sat down with them. A servant girl saw him seated there in the firelight. She looked closely at him and said, "This man was with him."
>
> But he denied it. "Woman, I don't know him," he said.
>
> A little later someone else saw him and said, "You also are one of them."
>
> "Man, I am not!" Peter replied.
>
> About an hour later another asserted, "Certainly this fellow was with him, for he is a Galilean."
>
> Peter replied, "Man, I don't know what you're talking about!" Just as he was speaking, the rooster crowed. The Lord turned and looked straight at Peter. Then Peter remembered the word the Lord had spoken to him: "Before the rooster crows today, you will disown me three times." And he went outside and wept bitterly. (Luke 22:54–62)

Peter absolutely deserved to be booted off the proverbial team and kicked to the curb during this low point in his life; instead, our resurrected Savior restored him (see John 21:15–17) and named him team captain. Peter never forgot the mercy Jesus lavished on him when he least deserved it, which fueled his passionate, world-changing faith for the rest of his life. I think it's fair to say that in the DNA of Christoformity is conscious and consistent gratitude for the wildly unmerited favor God gives mistake-prone ragamuffins like us.

- **WHY *CHRISTOFORMITY* MATTERS:** When someone puts their faith in Jesus Christ, they become a Christian, which means "little Christ." That name reveals our identity and our purpose—to become increasingly conformed into the image of our Savior . . . to live a Jesus-shaped life.

9

Christos

■ **CHRISTOS:** Comes from the Latin root word *christus,* which was transliterated as the Greek term *christos*. Prior to its use in the New Testament, *christos* referred to something that was "used as an ointment or salve" (related to *māšîaḥ* in Hebrew; see Exod. 28:41 and 1 Sam. 9:16). This is why the word *Christ* in our English New Testament translations technically means "Anointed One" or "Messiah."[1]

About a week or so after I brought Missy home from Haiti, we ran into a woman I knew—but not well—in the grocery store. She was very kind in congratulating me on finally becoming a mom through the miracle of adoption, then she focused her attention on Missy and asked sweetly, "What's your name, honey?" (She knew Missy's name but was trying to politely engage her in conversation.) Missy looked up at the woman with her big, beautiful brown eyes and responded in a very strong Creole accent, "Missy." To which the woman replied, "Well, that's a beautiful name. What's your last name, sweetie?"

Again, this kind acquaintance knew the gist of our story, so she knew that Missy's surname was now Harper. But Missy didn't know that. So concern clouded her precious little face because she knew this woman expected her to

1. Marinus de Jonge, "Christ," in *The Anchor Yale Bible Dictionary*, vol. 1, *A–C*, ed. David Noel Freedman (Doubleday, 1992), 914.

say something, but her English was limited, and she was tentative about talking to strangers. A few long seconds passed before Missy responded sincerely and slowly: "Mac-tur-tee" clearly emphasizing all three syllables. The woman tilted her head slightly and then glanced up at me as if to say, *What in the Sam Hill is she talking about?* And it took me a moment to explain because I had to stop laughing first. I didn't realize until right then and there that my habit of affectionately teasing Missy with silly nicknames like Tooter McGooder and Squirty McTurty throughout our two-year adoption process had left her a bit confused about what her real last name was.

The same can be said for many of us with regard to our Savior's "surname" because it's *not* Christ! In fact, most ancient Jews during the first century didn't even have hereditary last names like we use today (surnames didn't become common in Judaism until much later). Instead, God's people used *patronymics*, which identified them by their dad's name. That's why Jesus calls Peter "Simon son of Jonah" (Matt. 16:17). Although it's important to note that Jesus wasn't referred to as "Jesus *ben* Joseph" (*ben* means "son of" in Hebrew), except when He was being mocked (see John 6:42), more often than not our Messiah was identified by the village He grew up in: "Jesus of Nazareth" (Matt. 21:11; Mark 1:24; Luke 18:37; John 1:45; 19:19; Acts 2:22). Additionally, while the word *māšîaḥ* was used in the Old Testament to describe *anointing with* salve or oil, the related Hebrew word *mashiach* identified a ruler *who was anointed*, like King Saul or King David (see 2 Sam. 1:14; 19:21; Ps. 18:50), and *mashiach* is translated *Christos/Christ* in the Septuagint (the Greek translation of the Hebrew Scriptures). So, in the context of God's Word, "Christ" refers to a royal ruler instead of the surname someone might book a restaurant reservation under.

Now, just in case you've started tilting your head slightly because all this minutiae about monikers isn't making much sense, here's the bottom line: The word *christos* occurs about 350 times in the New Testament, and since it's usually found in connection to "Jesus Christ" and "Christ Jesus," it underscores the fact that Jesus is indeed the *Messiah*—the divine ruler and King of all kings

God's people had been praying about for centuries. Which is evidenced by Andrew's enthusiasm when he told his wary big brother Pete that he and a few of his buddies had met the *Messiah*:

> The next day John was there again with two of his disciples. When he saw Jesus passing by, he said, "Look, the Lamb of God!"
>
> When the two disciples heard him say this, they followed Jesus. Turning around, Jesus saw them following and asked, "What do you want?"
>
> They said, "Rabbi" (which means "Teacher"), "where are you staying?"
>
> "Come," he replied, "and you will see."
>
> So they went and saw where he was staying, and they spent that day with him. It was about four in the afternoon.
>
> Andrew, Simon Peter's brother, was one of the two who heard what John had said and who had followed Jesus. The first thing Andrew did was to find his brother Simon and tell him, "We have found the Messiah" (that is, the Christ). And he brought him to Jesus. (John 1:35–42)

Christ is infinitely more important than a surname, y'all. It means that Mary and Joe's baby boy who was born in a Bethlehem barn two thousand-ish years ago and then feted immediately afterward by shepherds—who discovered Jesus's shockingly humble birthing suite through the first "on-star" GPS navigation system—*is* the fulfillment of all the messianic promises:

1. *He was* a firstborn son, sanctified (Num. 3:13; Luke 2:7, 23).
2. *Kings did* bring Him gifts and fall down before Him (Ps. 72:10–11; Matt. 2:7–11).
3. *He was* born of a virgin (Isa. 7:13–14; Matt. 1:18–23).
4. *He was* born in Bethlehem of Judea (Mic. 5:2–5; Luke 2:4–7).
5. *He was* born a king, from the line of David (2 Sam. 7:12–13; Acts 13:22–23).
6. *Rulers did* take counsel against Him (Ps. 2:1–2; Matt. 26:3–4, 47).

7. *He did* speak in parables (Ps. 78:2; Matt. 13:34–35).
8. *He was* a caring shepherd (Isa. 40:1–11; John 10:14–15).
9. *He was* a priest after the order of Melchizedek (Ps. 110:4; Heb. 5:7–10).
10. *Someone did* prepare the way for Him (Isa. 40:3; John 1:21–27).
11. *He did* enter Jerusalem on a donkey (Zech. 9:9; John 12:13–15).
12. *He was* a Passover sacrifice without a bone broken (Num. 9:9–12; John 19:31–33).
13. *He was* lifted up—just as Moses lifted up a snake (Num. 21:8–9; John 3:14–15).
14. *He was* hung on a tree as a curse for us (Deut. 21:22–23; Gal. 3:13–14).
15. *He was* thirsty during His execution (Ps. 22:15; John 19:28).
16. *He was* given gall and vinegar/sour wine (Ps. 69:20–21; Luke 23:36).
17. *He was* sold for thirty pieces of silver (Zech. 11:12; Matt. 26:14–15).
18. The silver that betrayed Him *was used* to buy a potter's field (Zech. 11:13; Matt. 27:3–7).
19. *He was* struck on the cheek (Mic. 5:1; Matt. 27:30).
20. *He was* accused and afflicted but did not open His mouth (Isa. 53:7; Luke 23:8–9).

The apostle Paul, the most prominent writer in our New Testament canon, uses the word *Christos* almost three hundred times! It was obviously his favorite title for Jesus and—largely due to Paul's use of *Christos*/*Christ* in his epistles (all of which predate the four Gospel accounts)—it became the most common title by which believers refer to Jesus,[2] ultimately becoming the core of our identity as *Christ*ians or *Christ* followers.[3]

2. Joel B. Green, Jeannine K. Brown, and Nicholas Perrin, eds., *Dictionary of Jesus and the Gospels*, 2nd ed. (IVP Academic, 2013), under "Christ."
3. De Jonge, "Christ."

- **WHY *CHRISTOS* MATTERS:** This title represents a profound theological and historical significance that extends well beyond a surname. In the New Testament, the use of the title Christ (or *Christos* in the original Greek) places Jesus as the main hub of history, the one who ushers in a new age, and the Messiah sinners need to be redeemed and reconciled with a Holy God.

10

Covenant

■ **COVENANT:** Primarily defined as an agreement or pact between two parties, with particular significance in religious contexts.[1] In biblical terms, it often refers to the sacred agreements between God and humans, which were initiated and maintained by God. (There is also a specific Christian doctrine called "covenant theology," practiced primarily in the Reformed tradition, which identifies two main covenants in history: the "covenant of works" and the "covenant of grace."[2])

When I was six or seven years old, I pilfered a needle from the pin cushion beside Mom's sewing machine and met my backdoor neighbor and best friend, Terri, behind the bushes that camouflaged the chain-link fence between our homes. I don't remember exactly what I said during the oh-so-serious ceremony when we poked our thumb pads with the needle until little red dots appeared and then pressed our thumbs together to become "blood sisters," but it was probably along the lines of "This makes us family *forever*, and you will

1. Paul S. Karleen, *The Handbook to Bible Study: With a Guide to the Scofield Study System* (Oxford University Press, 1987), 318.
2. Douglas Mangum, *The Lexham Glossary of Theology* (Lexham Press, 2014), under "Covenant Theology."

always be my best friend." I do remember Terri's pale-faced, mute response, though, because she was more a gentle, let's-play-inside kind of child than an energetic tree-climbing tomboy like me, and my bloodletting idea just about put her over the edge. Not unlike the time I convinced her that guzzling an entire jar of pickle juice would be akin to drinking a beer (every now and then I chafed over the strict rules enforced by my dear Baptist-to-the-bone mama). The point I'm trying to make here (no pun intended) is that the promise I made after the pinprick could loosely be called a covenant or binding agreement. Now just imagine God's the one making the promise, which He did multiple times at the beginning of redemptive history.

He made a promise/covenant to protect Noah before the flood:

> I am going to bring floodwaters on the earth to destroy all life under the heavens, every creature that has the breath of life in it. Everything on earth will perish. *But I will establish my covenant with you,* and you will enter the ark—you and your sons and your wife and your sons' wives with you. (Gen. 6:17–18)

Then, after the flood, God makes a promise to protect Noah, his descendants, and all living creatures:

> And God said, "*This is the sign of the covenant I am making between me and you and every living creature with you, a covenant for all generations to come: I have set my rainbow in the clouds, and it will be the sign of the covenant between me and the earth.* Whenever I bring clouds over the earth and the rainbow appears in the clouds, *I will remember my covenant* between me and you and all living creatures of every kind. Never again will the waters become a flood to destroy all life. *Whenever the rainbow appears in the clouds, I will see it and remember the everlasting covenant between God and all living creatures of every kind on the earth.*"
>
> So God said to Noah, "This is the sign of the covenant I have established between me and all life on the earth." (Gen. 9:12–17)

After leading His people out of captivity in Egypt through a former murderer named Moses, God made a covenant with Israel, which was ratified by the Ten Commandments:

> On the first day of the third month after the Israelites left Egypt—on that very day—they came to the Desert of Sinai. After they set out from Rephidim, they entered the Desert of Sinai, and Israel camped there in the desert in front of the mountain.
>
> Then Moses went up to God, and the LORD called to him from the mountain and said, "This is what you are to say to the descendants of Jacob and what you are to tell the people of Israel: 'You yourselves have seen what I did to Egypt, and how I carried you on eagles' wings and brought you to myself. *Now if you obey me fully and keep my covenant, then out of all nations you will be my treasured possession.* Although the whole earth is mine, you will be for me a kingdom of priests and a holy nation.' These are the words you are to speak to the Israelites." (Exod. 19:1–6)

Our Creator Redeemer made another promise to a dude named David, whom God lovingly described as being "a man after his own heart" (1 Sam. 13:14) even though David didn't always keep *his* promises:

> "When your days are over and you rest with your ancestors, I will raise up your offspring to succeed you, your own flesh and blood, and I will establish his kingdom. He is the one who will build a house for my Name, and I will establish the throne of his kingdom forever. I will be his father, and he will be my son. When he does wrong, I will punish him with a rod wielded by men, with floggings inflicted by human hands. But my love will never be taken away from him, as I took it away from Saul, whom I removed from before you. Your house and your kingdom will endure forever before me; your throne will be established forever." . . .
>
> Sovereign LORD, you are God! *Your covenant is trustworthy,* and you have promised these good things to your servant. (2 Sam. 7:12–16, 28)

And my all-time favorite covenant God made with an Old Testament character was the binding agreement He established with Abraham, who'd already begun to doubt that God was going to fulfill a promise He'd made a few chapters earlier—in Genesis 12. That's when God promised that He was going to bless Abraham so that he could *be a blessing* (see Gen. 12:1–3) and went on to explain how Abraham and his wife, Sarah, were going to need to buy cases of Pampers even though they were both wearing Depends because they were *well past* the parenting stage of life:

> But Abram said, "Sovereign LORD, how can I know that I will gain possession of it?"
>
> So the LORD said to him, "Bring me a heifer, a goat and a ram, each three years old, along with a dove and a young pigeon."
>
> Abram brought all these to him, cut them in two and arranged the halves opposite each other; the birds, however, he did not cut in half. Then birds of prey came down on the carcasses, but Abram drove them away.
>
> As the sun was setting, Abram fell into a deep sleep, and a thick and dreadful darkness came over him. Then the LORD said to him, "Know for certain that for four hundred years your descendants will be strangers in a country not their own and that they will be enslaved and mistreated there. But I will punish the nation they serve as slaves, and afterward they will come out with great possessions. You, however, will go to your ancestors in peace and be buried at a good old age. In the fourth generation your descendants will come back here, for the sin of the Amorites has not yet reached its full measure."
>
> When the sun had set and darkness had fallen, *a smoking firepot with a blazing torch appeared and passed between the pieces*. On that day the LORD made a covenant with Abram and said, "To your descendants I give this land, from the Wadi of Egypt to the great river, the Euphrates—the land of the Kenites, Kenizzites, Kadmonites, Hittites, Perizzites, Rephaites, Amorites, Canaanites, Girgashites and Jebusites." (Gen. 15:8–21)

This ceremony is much more barbaric than the pinpricks Terri and I shared by the back fence—what with all the sliced-up animals and such—but you can tell by Abraham's compliance that he didn't think God's request was out of the ordinary. That's because using blood to ratify an agreement was a familiar ancient custom when two parties were making a pact.[3] Remember, pre-Canaanite society wasn't a literary culture—that means they didn't have written contracts—so their agreements were symbolized. And a blood covenant like the one God instructs Abe to prepare was the most binding of the ancient contracts because when an individual "passed between the pieces" of sacrificed animals, he was effectively saying to everyone witnessing the sober ceremony, "If I break this agreement, then may what was done to these animals be done to me."

The audacious miracle of this blood covenant our Creator made with Abraham is that *He* is the one who walked between the pieces, because the smoking firepot and the flaming torch are "theophanies"—they're physical manifestations of God Himself! By walking through alone, God was tangibly demonstrating, "If the covenant between us is broken, I'll pay the price in My blood." Of course, He knew we'd break our promises, that we'd follow our own selfish desires and resist His authority. He knew keeping the covenant was *completely* up to Him, which is why this colorful chapter in Genesis is like a massive finger pointing to the *new covenant* Jesus explained during the last meal He shared with His disciples:

> In the same way, after the supper he took the cup, saying, *"This cup is the new covenant in my blood, which is poured out for you."* (Luke 22:20)

Jesus's sacrificial death on a cross was the perfect collateral of the covenant God made with Abraham (who represented humanity)—our Savior fulfilled the merciful promise our heavenly Father had been making throughout redemptive history: *You* will *be My family forever.*

■ **WHY COVENANT MATTERS:** Covenants represent our Creator Redeemer's intentionality about redeeming and restoring humanity into an intimate relationship

3. Bill T. Arnold and Bryan E. Beyer, *Encountering the Old Testament* (Baker Books, 1999), 94.

with Himself. They are tangible signs of divine grace—of how God has consistently and compassionately inserted His redemptive plan throughout human history despite our rebellious tendencies. Not unlike the cairns (a small pile or tower of stones) hikers depend on to mark the path when they're navigating rocky territory that doesn't allow for signage, God's covenants mark the pathway of redemption that winds through biblical narrative.

11

Creedal Theology

■ **CREEDAL THEOLOGY:** The English word *creed* comes from the Latin word *credo*, which means "I believe." In the context of Christianity, a creed is a formal pledge of allegiance to a set of doctrinal statements concerning God and His relationship to humanity and creation. Therefore, creedal theology emphasizes the importance of ancient creeds like the Nicene Creed and the Apostles' Creed when it comes to shaping and understanding Christian belief and practice.

I graduated from Seminole High School in Central Florida in 1981—over *forty-five* years ago—but I can still warble (off-key, mind you—my sister got all the musical genes in our family!) our high school fight song. Because I sang those lyrics so many times with classmates at pep rallies and football games, they were pretty much engraved on my heart. I finished undergrad at Troy University in Alabama in 1985—over *forty* years ago—but I can still warble our Kappa Delta theme song. Because I sang those lyrics so many times with a close cadre of girlfriends, they were pretty much engraved on my heart too. There's something unifying and galvanizing about pledging your allegiance to something, along with a symphony of other voices pledging allegiance to the same thing. The collective chorus we hear with our ears reminds our hearts that we belong to something bigger than ourselves.

Creeds act like fertilizer on the flowers of community in the field of humanity.

Which is one of the main reasons some Christian churches incorporate creeds into their worship services. Although some people associate creeds solely with the theological statements/declarations written by the ancient spiritual leaders who established the doctrinal parameters for orthodox Christianity, creeds aren't just formal proclamations about our faith written by long-dead men. Short "statements of faith" are woven throughout Scripture—the divine revelation in which God *spoke*—which means He's the original proponent of creedal theology!

For instance, the Holy Spirit inspired Paul to use a creed in his first letter to the early church in Corinth:

> Now, brothers and sisters, *I want to remind you of the gospel I preached to you,* which you received and on which you have taken your stand. By this gospel you are saved, if you hold firmly to the word I preached to you. Otherwise, you have believed in vain.
>
> *For what I received I passed on to you as of first importance: that Christ died for our sins according to the Scriptures, that he was buried, that he was raised on the third day according to the Scriptures, and that he appeared to Cephas, and then to the Twelve. After that, he appeared to more than five hundred of the brothers and sisters at the same time, most of whom are still living, though some have fallen asleep. Then he appeared to James, then to all the apostles, and last of all he appeared to me also, as to one abnormally born.*
>
> For I am the least of the apostles and do not even deserve to be called an apostle, because I persecuted the church of God. But by the grace of God I am what I am, and his grace to me was not without effect. No, I worked harder than all of them—yet not I, but the grace of God that was with me. Whether, then, it is I or they, *this is what we preach, and this is what you believed.* (1 Cor. 15:1–11)

And the verse often used to explain the concept of salvation highlights the importance of creeds—of *professing* our faith:

> *If you declare with your mouth,* "Jesus is Lord," and believe in your heart that God raised him from the dead, you will be saved. (Rom. 10:9)

Now, just in case you still think creeds are reserved for certain denominations or are simply outdated, please keep reading! Most ancient Christians were illiterate. Our great-great-great-and-then-some spiritual ancestors didn't learn theology through books; they received verbal instruction from a spiritual leader. Converts were discipled for several weeks, months, or even years after confessing their faith in Jesus Christ prior to water baptism. This time of "learning the ropes" of Christianity was called *catechesis,* which is the Greek word for *teaching* and is why some churches still refer to "Christianity 101" learning as "catechism." So the first creeds declared in the New Testament church weren't the Nicene Creed or the Apostles' Creed (which came centuries later) but were instead the testimonies of new believers immediately before water baptism.

Furthermore, when those first Christians proclaimed a synopsis of what they'd learned in their "catechism classes" right before they were baptized, it wasn't a formal exercise or rote memorization—they were passionate, potentially life-threatening declarations! They were publicly shifting their allegiance from the pagan gods of Greco-Roman mythology to the one true God. They bravely bellowed those pre-baptism creeds in the nude, after which they were handed a white robe and a glass of milk and honey, symbolizing their arrival into the promised land.[1] Their proclamations made up the beautiful chorus of apostles, evangelists, missionaries, and martyrs who are now the great cloud of witnesses heralded in Hebrews 12:1.

I'm grateful the naked part is now stored in the museum of Christian history. But I hope Christ followers in modernity will choose to emulate our ancestors by harmonizing about our shared biblical beliefs instead of posting about our petty disagreements on social media. If it's been a while since you've spoken the Nicene Creed out loud (the following version is more accurately known

1. Litfin, *Story of the Trinity*, 23.

as the Niceno-Constantinopolitan Creed because it was revised at the Council of Constantinople in AD 381), I encourage you to do so. Better yet, gather a couple of friends and do so with unified gusto!

> We believe in one God, the Father All Governing, creator of heaven and earth, of all things visible and invisible.
>
> And in one Lord Jesus Christ, the only-begotten Son of God, begotten from the Father before all time, Light from Light, true God from true God, begotten not created, of the same essence as the Father, through Whom all things came into being; Who for us men and because of our salvation came down from heaven, and was incarnate by the Holy Spirit and the Virgin Mary and became human. He was crucified for us under Pontius Pilate, and suffered and was buried, and rose on the third day, according to the Scriptures, and ascended to heaven, and sits on the right hand of the Father, and will come again with glory to judge the living and dead. His kingdom shall have no end.
>
> And in the Holy Spirit, the Lord and life-giver, Who proceeds from the Father, Who is worshiped and glorified together with the Father and Son, Who spoke through the prophets; and in one, holy, catholic, and apostolic Church. We confess one baptism for the remission of sins. We look forward to the resurrection of the dead and the life of the world to come. Amen.[2]

■ **WHY *CREEDAL THEOLOGY* MATTERS:** Because, much like CliffsNotes that condense the key points of a book or the note cards students use to prepare for a test, creeds synopsize and elucidate the most important doctrines of our Christian belief system. Therefore, they can be very effective and accurate reminders of the foundational walls of biblical orthodoxy. The public confession of Christian creeds also forges unity among Christ followers.

---

2. John H. Leith, ed., *Creeds of the Churches*, 3rd ed. (Westminster John Knox, 1982), 33.

12

The Day of the Lord

- **THE DAY OF THE LORD:** The time of the decisive visitation of God, when He intervenes to punish the wicked, deliver and exalt the faithful remnant who worship Him, and establish His own rule. Both judgment and salvation are especially prominent aspects. The Day of the Lord is a significant concept in biblical eschatology, especially in the Old Testament prophetic books. Though the precise term appears only sixteen times in the Old Testament, other temporal phrases are clearly relevant (e.g., "the LORD Almighty has a day in store," Isa. 2:12; "in the day of the LORD's wrath," Ezek. 7:19; "in that day," Amos 8:9; "on the day of the LORD's sacrifice," Zeph. 1:8; "on that day," Zeph. 1:9–10). Some scholars consider this to be the central theme of the entire prophetic message; the books of Joel and Zephaniah are completely devoted to proclaiming the Day of the Lord and its attendant events.[1]

My little brother—who's eight years younger than me—was a very energetic little boy who was equal parts mischievous imp and blond-haired, blue-eyed

1. Greg A. King, "Day of the Lord," in *Eerdmans Dictionary of the Bible*, ed. David Noel Freedman, Allen C. Myers, and Astrid B. Beck (Eerdmans, 2000), 324.

cherub. Needless to say, the mischievous part of him pulled the wee angel part into lots of trouble! I'll never forget the time he swiped a dozen or so little enamel pins depicting cars, animals, and sports teams from the counter display at the mom-and-pop grocery store a few blocks from our house, then proudly displayed them on the brim of his ball cap. He was probably six or seven years old at the time and was always asking Mom to buy him a pin when we went to the store. But we didn't have much discretionary money back then, so while she bought him a few, most of the time she had to gently refuse his request.

However, one night when we were all watching *The Waltons* on TV in the living room, I watched Mom's eyes rest on my brother's hat. She noted the pins on the brim, and when she asked him how he'd managed to amass such a large collection, his panicked expression betrayed his guilt. But then his countenance quickly shifted, and he began to wail with remorse over his "sin" and between shaking sobs cried that he was *so ashamed!* Of course, by then our mom was wise to my little brother's persuasive antics and didn't buy his Oscar-worthy confession. Instead, she snatched him up by the back of the collar, bundled him into the car, drove him down to the store, and made him confess to the owner and give back every single pin he'd pilfered. He also had to pay back the cost of what he'd stolen with birthday/Christmas/chore money. My mother, Patti Angel, did not play—when she found out one of her kids had lied, stolen, been disrespectful, or disobeyed her rules in any form or fashion, there was heck to pay, honey!

Scripture makes it clear that God doesn't play either, and there will be a point when unrepentant sinners have much more than heck to pay, which is chillingly clear in this prophetic warning from Zephaniah:

> Be silent before the Sovereign LORD,
> for *the day of the LORD is near*.
> The LORD has prepared a sacrifice;
> he has consecrated those he has invited.

"On the day of the Lord's sacrifice
I will punish the officials
and the king's sons
and all those clad
in foreign clothes.
On that day I will punish
all who avoid stepping on the threshold,
who fill the temple of their gods
with violence and deceit.

"On that day,"
declares the LORD,
"a cry will go up from the Fish Gate,
wailing from the New Quarter,
and a loud crash from the hills.
Wail, you who live in the market district;
all your merchants will be wiped out,
all who trade with silver will be destroyed.
At that time I will search Jerusalem with lamps
and punish those who are complacent,
who are like wine left on its dregs,
who think, 'The LORD will do nothing,
either good or bad.'
Their wealth will be plundered,
their houses demolished.
Though they build houses,
they will not live in them;
though they plant vineyards,
they will not drink the wine."

The great day of the Lord is near—
near and coming quickly.
The cry on the day of the Lord is bitter;
the Mighty Warrior shouts his battle cry.

That day will be a day of wrath—
  a day of distress and anguish,
    a day of trouble and ruin,
  a day of darkness and gloom,
    a day of clouds and blackness—
  a day of trumpet and battle cry
against the fortified cities
  and against the corner towers.

"I will bring such distress on all people
  that they will grope about like those who are blind,
  because they have sinned against the LORD.
Their blood will be poured out like dust
  and their entrails like dung.
Neither their silver nor their gold
  will be able to save them
  on the day of the LORD's wrath."

In the fire of his jealousy
  the whole earth will be consumed,
for he will make a sudden end
  of all who live on the earth. (Zeph. 1:7–18)

The little boy of a good friend of mine used to race upstairs and put on a second pair of pants when he got in trouble so he'd have extra padding if his dad decided to spank him, and I bet that's what the Israelites were tempted to do as well when they heard Zephaniah's sermon. His "Day of the Lord" warning has two alarming applications; the first involves the punitive consequences the people in Judah will face as a result of their sin. And second, there's a foreboding omen for the entire world in verse 18: "He will make a sudden end of all who live on the earth." In other words, there will come a point in time where *everybody* has to pay up.

Thankfully, there's a glimmer of good news with regard to the coming "Day of the Lord" as well, because this goose bump–inducing phraseology also points ahead to the gospel of Jesus Christ, God's gracious antidote for habitual rebellion:

> *But the day of the Lord will come like a thief.* The heavens will disappear with a roar; the elements will be destroyed by fire, and the earth and everything done in it will be laid bare. . . .
>
> Therefore, dear friends, since you have been forewarned, be on your guard so that you may not be carried away by the error of the lawless and fall from your secure position. But grow in the grace and knowledge of our Lord and Savior Jesus Christ. To him be glory both now and forever! Amen. (2 Pet. 3:10, 17–18)

- **WHY *THE DAY OF THE LORD* MATTERS:** Warnings are important because, much like a yield sign on the highway, they keep us from swerving off the road and being injured in some kind of spiritual wreck. Additionally, the looming "Day of the Lord" serves to remind Christ followers to stay tethered to the Word of God, keep in step with the Holy Spirit, and forge authentic and accountable relationships. A healthy awareness of future judgment also provides motivation to live righteously and a framework for human suffering.

13

The Dead Sea Scrolls

- **THE DEAD SEA SCROLLS:** A collection of ancient documents—dating from around 300 BC to AD 40—that were discovered in caves near Qumran in the Judean Desert between 1947 and 1956. These scrolls include texts from the Hebrew Bible, other holy books, commentaries, and community rules. Some scholars consider the Dead Sea Scrolls one of the greatest literary and archaeological discoveries of our time because they're effectively a well-preserved scrapbook of ancient Judaism and early Christianity. The scrolls contain copies of all Old Testament books except Esther, as well as nonbiblical texts like the War Scroll and the Temple Scroll.[1] Unfortunately, because unscrupulous people have sold expensive forgeries of the Dead Sea Scrolls to legitimate museums and collectors, the veracity of the legitimate scrolls has sometimes been questioned in modernity.

In the late 1940s a Syrian boy was herding his goats near Qumran—John the Baptist's old neighborhood near the Dead Sea—when he threw a rock to try and get one of his stray goats to come down from a rocky hill it had ascended. The stone he hurled made an interesting shattering sound because unbeknownst to him it had broken a large water jar in which some very important religious

1. Craig S. Keener, *The IVP Bible Background Commentary: New Testament* (InterVarsity, 1993), 780.

writings (scrolls) had been stored for thousands of years. The boy, Muhammed edh-Dhib (edh-Dhib means "the Wolf"), was initially frightened and ran away. But curiosity got the better of him and he came back later with his cousin, scrambled up the hill, explored the shallow cave where his rock had landed, and discovered ancient manuscripts inscribed on leather and papyrus that soon became known as the first of the Dead Sea Scrolls.[2]

The scrolls—which now number almost one thousand, as many more were discovered—date back to as early as the third century BC all the way up to AD 68. That Bedouin boy's accidental discovery is now considered one of the more important finds in the history of modern archaeology, and it's especially important for Christ followers because the Dead Sea Scrolls are hundreds of years older than previously known biblical manuscripts and authenticate the historicity, accuracy, and trustworthiness of Scripture. Prior to their discovery, the oldest copy of the Hebrew Scriptures (the Masoretic Text) is from the ninth century AD, and our earliest version of the Septuagint (abbreviated LXX; the Greek translation of the Hebrew Scriptures) is from the third century AD.

Furthermore, the Latin Vulgate (the first Latin translation of both the Old and New Testaments, which was transcribed by Saint Jerome) is from the fourth century AD. In other words, prior to the discovery of the Dead Sea Scrolls it was presumed that the Koran/Quran (the religious text of Islam) predated the Christian Bible. But the scrolls effectively refute that presumption, prove the Old Testament we have now was in fact the very Bible Jesus studied, and verify that the words of God our heavenly Father—Abba—were breathed long before the teachings of Allah.

What makes that Arabic adolescent's discovery even more special, in my opinion, is that while the land of Israel has been teeming with archaeologists for centuries because its climate and soil are advantageous when it comes to preserving ancient artifacts, it wasn't some brilliant Indiana Jones type who

2. Edmund Wilson, "The Scrolls from the Dead Sea," *The New Yorker*, May 6, 1955, https://www.newyorker.com/magazine/1955/05/14/the-scrolls-from-the-dead-sea.

found the first Dead Sea Scrolls. Instead, our Creator Redeemer revealed His inscripturated words—which had been written and then hidden away in those caves for safekeeping by ancient scribes who some scholars believe were a monastic group called the Essenes, with whom John the Baptist was associated during his ministry in the Judean wilderness—to a *shepherd boy*! Which can't help but remind us of how God first revealed Jesus, His only begotten Son—whom John's Gospel account refers to as the Living Word (John 1:1)—to another group of humble shepherds not too far down the road from Qumran in a dusty town called Bethlehem:

> *And there were shepherds living out in the fields nearby*, keeping watch over their flocks at night. An angel of the Lord appeared to them, and the glory of the Lord shone around them, and they were terrified. But the angel said to them, "Do not be afraid. I bring you good news that will cause great joy for all the people. Today in the town of David a Savior has been born to you; he is the Messiah, the Lord. This will be a sign to you: You will find a baby wrapped in cloths and lying in a manger." (Luke 2:8–12)

Contrary to the darling bathrobe-clad children we've seen playing the part of shepherds in Christmas plays, real first-century shepherds didn't compel adults to ooh and aah and snap pictures. Because not only were they illiterate nomads, they were stinky because they slept outside with sheep and goats! Plus, by the time Jesus's earthly ministry was established, herding animals was no longer a reputable family business like it had been during the Old Testament era (see 1 Sam. 16:11); instead, shepherds were synonymous with uncleanliness and thievery. They were so low in the social strata that the Talmud (the primary source of Jewish law) declared shepherds too unreliable to be credible witnesses in court. People in the ancient Near East needed shepherds to take care of their animals—maybe to clean out their barns—but they certainly wouldn't have been invited to a party, much less as the first guests of a royal birth.

Interestingly enough, Muhammed edh-Dhib's family were considered "low-lifes" in their culture too. They earned a bad reputation for avoiding customs officers at the Israeli border and smuggling their goats and other goods into Bethlehem to sell at the black market. Which is where, in 1947, they sought out a Jewish merchant who bought and sold ancient artifacts. However, when they offered the merchant those initial Dead Sea Scrolls for twenty pounds—about $2,600 nowadays—he refused to buy them because he couldn't read the ancient Hebrew written on them, he was put off by the Wolf family's rough and dirty exterior, and he presumed the scrolls to be worthless. The shepherding Wolf clan was eventually able to find another buyer a few months later, and while the price of those first Dead Sea Scrolls has never been made public, it's rumored they were sold for fifty pounds—about $6,500 today.

Of course, modern archaeologists, antiquities experts, and museum directors won't even attempt to estimate the value of the authenticated Dead Sea Scrolls now because they're considered priceless in terms of their spiritual, archaeological, and historical value.

- **WHY *THE DEAD SEA SCROLLS* MATTER:** These ancient artifacts prove the historicity, accuracy, and trustworthiness of the Holy Scriptures. They confirm the Old Testament we read today is the very same one our Savior studied when He was a boy growing up in Nazareth and when He was an itinerate rabbi. And they verify that the Christian Bible predates the Koran/Quran (the religious text of Islam).

14

Ecclesiology

ECCLESIOLOGY: Comes from two Greek words—*ekklēsia,* which means "assembly," and *logos,* which means "word"; therefore, *ecclesiology* means "the study of the church." It is the theological discipline that considers the nature, mission, and structure of the Christian church.[1] It encompasses various aspects, including the church's foundation, purpose, and identity through history and in the present.[2]

I've had the undeserved privilege of worshiping Jesus in well over a thousand different churches around the world, which has been an extraordinary gift because I'm a church girl through and through. I like megachurches and tiny churches; loud churches and quiet churches; hipster churches that meet in coffee shops or movie theaters and are presided over by pastors with lots of tattoos; and formal churches that meet in sanctuaries filled with gleaming wooden pews flanked by stained-glass windows and are presided over by robe-wearing spiritual leaders. I've been in vocational ministry for almost forty years, and I've rarely met a church I didn't like—at least in part—because

1. Paul Avis, *Reshaping Ecumenical Theology: The Church Made Whole?* (T&T Clark, 2010), 142.
2. Paul Avis, "Ecclesiology," in *The Oxford Dictionary of the Christian Church,* ed. Andrew Louth (Oxford University Press, 2022), 602.

even when I've found myself in a less-than-welcoming congregation, there's always been at least one kind saint who has offered me a smile and prompted me to ponder, *If we lived in the same city, I bet we'd be friends.* Which begs the question: What makes a church? Is it defined by a building, or is it defined by the mistake-prone people who gather in that space to worship God?

We can look to the first Christian church, which formed on the heels of the crucifixion and resurrection of Jesus Christ and is chronicled in the New Testament book of Acts, to effectively answer the question:

> Peter replied, "Repent and be baptized, every one of you, in the name of Jesus Christ for the forgiveness of your sins. And you will receive the gift of the Holy Spirit. The promise is for you and your children and for all who are far off—for all whom the Lord our God will call."
>
> With many other words he warned them; and he pleaded with them, "Save yourselves from this corrupt generation." Those who accepted his message were baptized, and about three thousand were added to their number that day.
>
> *They devoted themselves to the apostles' teaching and to fellowship, to the breaking of bread and to prayer.* Everyone was filled with awe at the many wonders and signs performed by the apostles. All the believers were together and had everything in common. They sold property and possessions to give to anyone who had need. Every day they continued to meet together in the temple courts. They broke bread in their homes and ate together with glad and sincere hearts, praising God and enjoying the favor of all the people. And the Lord added to their number daily those who were being saved. (Acts 2:38–47)

Luke's initial church narrative doesn't mention anything about the architectural style or square footage of *where* our Christian ancestors met, but he makes it abundantly clear *why* they met. They gathered to focus their attention and affection on God and to celebrate communion together and remember the miraculous sufficiency of Jesus's sacrificial death and bodily resurrection—how His ministry reconciled sinners like them into a right relationship with Holy

God. They also gathered to engage in real, compassionate relationships: "All the believers lived in a wonderful harmony, holding everything in common" (Acts 2:44 MSG). Their worship "service" expressed devotion to God *and* to each other: "They followed a daily discipline of worship in the Temple followed by meals at home" (Acts 2:46 MSG). Plus, their church was a joyful place to hang out: "Every meal a celebration, exuberant and joyful, as they praised God" (Acts 2:46 MSG). It's no wonder their congregation was growing like a weed! What started out as 120 believers at the beginning of Acts (1:15) quickly swelled to 3,120 following Pete's first sermon (Acts 2:41) and then exploded to 8,120 congregants *while* Pete was being dragged off to jail as a result of his second sermon (Acts 4:4)! Not unlike a Walmart on the morning after Thanksgiving, the first Christian church was *the place* to gather after the resurrection and ascension of Jesus.

Luke goes on to describe the first notes of the early church as a gorgeous symphony of healthy interdependency:

> *All the believers were one in heart and mind. No one claimed that any of their possessions was their own, but they shared everything they had. With great power the apostles continued to testify to the resurrection of the Lord Jesus. And God's grace was so powerfully at work in them all that there were no needy persons among them. For from time to time those who owned land or houses sold them, brought the money from the sales and put it at the apostles' feet, and it was distributed to anyone who had need.*
>
> Joseph, a Levite from Cyprus, whom the apostles called Barnabas (which means "son of encouragement"), sold a field he owned and brought the money and put it at the apostles' feet. (Acts 4:32–37)

Their church wasn't defined by a building, what day or time of day they met, whether they raised their hands or sat on them during worship, or what they wore when they gathered. Instead, the original parameters of Christian congregation were *power* (from the Greek word *dynamis,* which means "force or boldness")—their faith was strengthened from the teaching and testimonies of the disciples—and *grace* (from the Greek word *charis*, which means "unmerited favor")—their love for God and each other was fertilized in that miraculous, motley crew of saved sinners. Plus, their power and grace were palpable because they captured the attention of the world around them and prompted new believers to join their family of faith every single day (Acts 2:47).

The first church was:

- A safe place to learn more about our Creator Redeemer through teaching, worship, prayer, discipleship, and celebrating the sacraments of baptism and communion
- A safe place for the poor, weak, and sick to lean on the combined strength of Christian community
- A safe place to be launched on mission as Christ's ambassadors to the world around us

It's no wonder our Creator Redeemer encourages His church to keep meeting, and all the more as the second advent of Jesus Christ approaches (see Heb. 10:24–25).

■ **WHY *ECCLESIOLOGY* MATTERS:** Because it reminds us that God, not man, is the master church planner! Instead of leaning solely on human wisdom, strategy, and cultural trends, we must also consider how gatherings of God's people have best been used for His kingdom purposes throughout two thousand years of Christian history. Biblically informed ecclesiology can go a long way in helping modern houses of worship develop and maintain healthy internal structures, interdependent relationships within their local body, effective care for the poor, and positive, Christoformic impact on their local community.

15

Eisegesis

EISEGESIS: The interpretation of a text (as of the Bible) by reading into it one's own ideas.[1]

During my first go-round in seminary, when I was studying for a master's in theological studies, I had a professor who often teasingly told his students, "Keep your *I*'s out of exegesis!" He explained that *eisegesis* was the dangerous opposite of *exegesis*—whereby we prayerfully and responsibly *draw knowledge out* of Scripture—because instead of letting God's Word *read us, eisegesis* means reading our agendas and biases *into Holy Writ*. He strongly encouraged us to let our Creator Redeemer's supernatural, inscripturated revelation speak for itself instead of imposing our preconceived ideas onto it or even trying to "defend" the veracity of God's Word to its detractors. Charles Spurgeon preached a similar assertion in a sermon titled "Christ and His Co-Workers": "Never mind about defending Deuteronomy or the whole of the Pentateuch; preach Jesus Christ and him crucified. Let the Lion out, and see who will

1. *Merriam-Webster Dictionary*, "eisegesis," accessed October 14, 2025, https://www.merriam-webster.com/dictionary/eisegesis.

dare to approach him. The Lion of the tribe of Judah will soon drive away all his adversaries."[2]

Let the Lion of Judah out. That statement still makes my heart stand up straight in respectful attention. Why in the world do we humans foolishly feel the need to try and tame the Lion of Judah into a declawed tabby caged by our preferences and limited understanding? Goodness gracious, sometimes we need to be shaken from our spiritual stupor! Which reminds me of a jarring situation I found myself in many years ago.

I'd accepted an invitation to teach at a women's conference (I'm so grateful for the undeserved privilege of getting to talk about the unconditional love of Jesus Christ, and every invitation still makes me feel like I got asked to prom by the quarterback of the football team!) and was told by the conference leadership team that they'd picked Psalm 42 as the theme of the entire event. So I spent a lot of time studying Psalm 42 beforehand. I deeply appreciate the raw emotion, vulnerability, and relatability of the Psalms—John Calvin described them as "an anatomy of all parts of the soul"[3]—but I was a tad surprised they'd picked Psalm 42 as the sole focus of their women's gathering because it's a psalm of lament, which means it's a *sad* song (all of the Psalms were originally written as songs).

It was written by the sons of Korah, who led musical worship both in the tent of meeting—which was where the Israelites worshiped before they had a brick-and-mortar building—and then in the temple when it was constructed (1 Chron. 6:16, 31–48; 2 Chron. 20:19). But these ancient warblers were looking in the rearview mirror when they penned this melancholy tune because it describes a season when they're no longer leading an ancient choir of God's

2. Charles Haddon Spurgeon, "Christ and His Co-Workers," *Metropolitan Tabernacle Pulpit,* vol. 42, The Spurgeon Center for Biblical Preaching at Midwestern Seminary, June 10, 1886, https://www.spurgeon.org/resource-library/sermons/christ-and-his-co-workers/#flipbook/.

3. John Calvin, "The Author's Preface," *Commentary on Psalms,* vol. 1, Christian Classics Ethereal Library, Calvin University, accessed October 28, 2025, https://www.ccel.org/ccel/calvin/calcom08.vi.html.

people and they've lost their spiritual groove and feel like they're drowning in grief, as evidenced by the following lyrics:

> My soul thirsts for God, for the living God.
> When can I go and meet with God?
> *My tears have been my food*
> *day and night,*
> while people say to me all day long,
> "Where is your God?" . . .
>
> *My soul is downcast within me;*
> therefore I will remember you
> from the land of the Jordan,
> the heights of Hermon—from Mount Mizar.
> Deep calls to deep
> in the roar of your waterfalls;
> *all your waves and breakers*
> *have swept over me.* (Ps. 42:2–3, 6–7)

This psalm ends on a redemptive "up" note (Psalm 82 is the only psalm of lament that doesn't), but I'm so glad God's Word includes this kind of unflinching honesty. Instead of making disillusioned people feel disowned, Psalm 42 is like our Creator Redeemer's engraved invitation for us to bring Him *all* of our emotions, not just the happy-clappy ones. It proves we don't have to curate our feelings into acceptable and unacceptable piles for God. This poignant confession in the middle of our Bibles illustrates that the first step to getting our groove back might just be admitting we've lost it.

Unfortunately, I don't think too many women at that conference felt safe enough to express their heartache and waning hope because the leaders had unwittingly let *eisegesis* take over the decorating committee. That meant we were all handed Hawaiian leis and chocolate-covered macadamia nuts by happy, grass-skirt-wearing volunteers when we entered the convention center.

And it was hard to hear the worship songs or Bible teaching because the noise from the gorgeous, working—albeit wildly out of context—waterfall they'd had a crew of hapless husbands construct on the stage drowned everything else out!

Eisegesis might not sound like a big deal, but it can sure muddy the waters of what God intended for us to take away from His Word.

- **WHY *EISEGESIS* MATTERS:** Eisegesis matters because it can impose external meaning—like human preference or prejudice—on a biblical text where that was not the original author's intent. When we filter the Word of God through the minds, mouths, and laptops of mere humans, of course it's going to be distorted at some level. However, we must determine to understand and apply the divine promises and parameters of the Holy Scriptures as closely to our Creator Redeemer's intent as possible.

16

Epignosis

▪ **EPIGNOSIS:** *Gnosis,* the Greek word for *knowledge,* is here preceded by the preposition *epi,* which means "toward," or "in the direction of." Therefore, *epignosis* can be interpreted as knowledge that is always moving closer in the direction of who/what it seeks to know.[1]

Epignosis, which can be loosely defined as "heart knowledge," isn't as common in the New Testament canon as *gnosis,* or "head knowledge," perhaps because it's used primarily in the context of a real relationship—of *knowing* Jesus, not just *knowing about* Jesus. My favorite quote that reads like a synopsis of epignosis—often attributed to Blaise Pascal, one of my favorite theologians and deep thinkers from the 1600s—is "Things human must be known to be loved; things divine must be loved to be known."

I wanted to make the first Christmas Missy was home from Haiti extra special, so I blocked out several weeks in December just for the two of us and planned a plethora of Advent activities. However, since our adoption transition counselor warned me that Missy's senses could easily be overwhelmed by what we consider "traditional" here in America, I planned mostly intimate,

1. "The All-Important Knowledge (2 Peter 1:2)," *Barclay's Daily Study Bible,* StudyLight.org, accessed December 3, 2025, https://www.studylight.org/commentaries/eng/dsb/2-peter-1.html.

relatively quiet ways to celebrate, like baking cookies, slowly decorating the tree, dribbling dozens of icicles on gingerbread houses, watching old holiday movies, and going for long drives almost every night to look at Christmas lights and sing carols in the car. Everything went exactly the way I imagined it until the week before Christmas.

We discovered a new neighborhood to drive through that was especially dressed up with what seemed to be a million lights, which was a big first-Christmas-home-with-mom hit. Plus, we'd enjoyed a really yummy dinner at the Asian restaurant Missy picked out (she loves "sissy sushi"—the kind with tempura shrimp—and Pad Thai and had enjoyed both at this particular restaurant before), which was also a big first-Christmas-home-with-mom hit. But she started looking a little puny on the drive home, so I put her in my bed instead of upstairs in hers in order to keep a close eye on her. Of course, I couldn't sleep the first few hours after she nodded off because I was worried that she was getting sick. I kept feeling her forehead every so often to see if she had a fever and finally fell asleep myself around 2:00 a.m. But something jostled my mama heart awake at 3:00 a.m.—it's weirdly awesome how our internal parenting radar *just knows* when our kids aren't okay even if we're unconscious—and I sat straight up in bed, then immediately reached for her forehead with one hand while I fumbled for the switch on the bedside lamp with the other.

Panic shot through me because her forehead was wet, but before the light illuminated the room, I knew it wasn't perspiration from fever that my baby girl was wearing. My guess is that all those shrimp she gobbled were forced to sit in the back of a truck for far too long on their journey from the coast to landlocked Tennessee, which made them very resentful. So when they staged a mutiny to leave Missy's body, they flew out with a fiery vengeance. I'll spare you the details except to say I had to throw my bed linens and comforter *out the back door into the yard* to deal with later, take down my curtains, scrub walls, and spend a great deal of time holding my screaming, squirming child in the shower in order to pick all the stinky shrimp remnants out of her beautiful curly hair with tweezers. When I threw the final dirty towel over the porch rail into the yard (yes, they were *that* dirty), my brain blinked its groggy eyes in surprise that the sun was up. Then the alarm on my phone went off, and I realized with a groan that Missy's babysitter was coming over soon because I was booked to speak at a women's Christmas brunch in downtown Nashville that morning.

A couple of hours later I was standing in the back of a beautifully decorated hotel conference center next to my dear friend Pepper—who'd helped host the event—greeting women as they left. When there was a pause in the flow of people leaving, she looked at me closely and said, "Lease, you look tired." So I told her about the projectile "vomit-arrhea-tastrophe." When I finished describing the ordeal, she patted my arm with palpable empathy. Pepper has six children and is well-acquainted with what I'd experienced for the first time. Then she said in a slow, sweet, and sincere Southern drawl, "Well, honey, I know you didn't have to have an episiotomy to bring Missy into this world, but anyone who's had to clean number two off walls and out of their child's hair is *officially* a mother."

I read stacks of books on parenting before bringing Missy home from Haiti and saved everything that sounded like important information in files on my laptop and mentally filed them away in my brain. I didn't realize then that the stuff I really needed to *know* about being her second mama had to be experienced firsthand, next to her. That's when it went from conceptual to concrete—to something my heart could hold on to. I think that's the kind of real, roll-your-sleeves-up-and-get-your-hands-dirty-in-an-intimate-relationship kind of *heart knowledge* Paul encouraged the young Christians in Colossae to develop with God:

> For this reason, since the day we heard about you, we have not stopped praying for you. We continually ask God to fill you with the *knowledge* [epignosis/heart knowledge] of his will through all the wisdom and understanding that the Spirit gives, so that you may live a life worthy of the Lord and please him in every way: bearing fruit in every good work, growing in the *knowledge*

> [epignosis/heart knowledge] of God, being strengthened with all power according to his glorious might so that you may have great endurance and patience, and giving joyful thanks to the Father, who has qualified you to share in the inheritance of his holy people in the kingdom of light. (Col. 1:9–12)

It's not enough to accumulate information about God in your brain; you've got to know Him with your heart too.

- **WHY *EPIGNOSIS* MATTERS:** Epignosis illustrates how a reader of God's Word can become an active participant in His redemption story because it expresses both an understanding of our heavenly Father's will and the desire to model what He mandates. In modern Christian vernacular, this is sometimes referred to as walking what you talk or practicing what you preach. Epignosis occurs when our *orthodoxy* (what we believe to be true of God) informs and transforms our *orthopraxy* (how we live in light of what we believe to be true of God).

17

Eschatology

ESCHATOLOGY: Derived from the Greek word *eschatos*, meaning "last" or "final," eschatology is teaching about "the last things."[1]

In other words, eschatology is a theological viewpoint or field of study that focuses on the final outworking of God's purposes and activity, as well as our ultimate human destiny. Given the fact that eschatology isn't an exact science, doctrinal beliefs vary widely based on differing interpretations of prophetic passages in Scripture, which are prominent in books like Isaiah, Jeremiah, Ezekiel, Daniel, and Revelation but can be found scattered throughout the Bible. Additionally, there are two poles of application with regard to the study of eschatology: *personal eschatology*, which refers to where we believe we'll go when we die, heaven or hell; and *cosmic eschatology*, which refers to what will happen to the world when time as we know it ends.[2] Eschatology is surely a deep, seemingly bottomless pool to ponder, and when you can't see the bottom, it can be a little scary.

1. David L. Petersen, George W. E. Nickelsburg, and D. E. Aune, "Eschatology," in *The Anchor Yale Bible Dictionary*, vol. 2, *D–G*, ed. David Noel Freedman (Doubleday, 1992), 575.

2. Fred Sanders, "The Doctrine of the Last Things," in *Lexham Survey of Theology*, ed. Mark Ward, Jessica Parks, Brannon Ellis, and Todd Hains (Lexham Press, 2018), Logos edition.

Recently, Missy and I were walking down to the dock to go for a late afternoon ride on our Jet Ski when a neighbor walking up from the dock waved us over with a serious look on his face. He said, "Hey y'all, be careful down there because we just saw a huge copperhead snake by the Jet Ski ports." Then he added reassuringly, "Thank goodness it wasn't a cottonmouth because those things are deadly poisonous—if you get bitten by one, you need to get to the hospital as fast as you can. But copperhead bites are rarely lethal. I mean, they hurt like the dickens, but you probably won't die from it."

I swallowed the panic rising from my toes to the top of my head (because I really, *really* hate snakes) before asking with false calm, "I assume copperheads have rust-colored heads, but what does the rest of their body look like?"

He explained that they were usually taupe or bronze with markings similar to a rattlesnake or python.

We should've done an about-face and hightailed it in the opposite direction of the slithery but probably-won't-kill-you critter. However, Missy had been such a trooper with my intense workload and travel schedule, and all she'd asked me for was a little downtime at the lake, so we kept walking toward the water. By the time we got to the dock, I was high-stepping like a show pony so my feet didn't rest on the ground for too long (because I'd heard snakes tend to strike low), and we were making as much noise as possible (because I'd heard noise/vibration drives them away), but just as we were approaching our ski, I saw the coiled monster directly in front of it. I threw my arm in front of Missy protectively and screamed so loud that our neighbor came running back to the dock before realizing the "snake" was just a towrope someone had left behind after a day of tubing.

Because I'd been previously warned about a big, scary snake, my mind was anxiously primed to see one. Which is all too often the case with eschatology. Because of the plethora of ominous movies, books, and sermons on the subject matter of the end times, some folks understandably get nervous when a street address or phone number includes three sixes in a row, let alone when we hear news reports about people getting microchips inserted on the tops of their hands as a newfangled form of payment!

Although there are lots of gaps in our human understanding about the end times (remember, even our Savior said He doesn't know all the details regarding His second coming—"But about that day or hour no one knows, not even the angels in heaven, nor the Son, but only the Father" [Mark 13:32]), if you've put your hope in Jesus, you don't have to be afraid. Because what we can understand from far less bewildering biblical truisms is that He came to earth in incarnate form, the Spirit of the living God was poured out, and after Jesus died on a cross for our sins, He rose from the dead to take His place at the right hand of God the Father, where He now sits enthroned and interceding on our behalf. Therefore, while eschatology reflects on the "final chapter" of human history, the supernaturally happy ending has already been assured. Scary isn't looming around the corner; being reunited with our risen Savior is!

- **WHY *ESCHATOLOGY* MATTERS:** Eschatology matters because it sets the entire reality of Creation, the Fall, the first advent (the incarnation of Jesus), and the second advent (when our Savior returns to claim His bride, the Christian church) into a redemptive metanarrative. A biblically sound doctrine of the "last" or "final" things puts the entire human experience under God's divine umbrella of grace. It clarifies that our Creator had a plan for restoring and reconciling us to Himself through faith in Jesus all along, and God's divine plan will be perfectly consummated when we get to step into His unconditionally loving, trinitarian presence in Glory. Eschatology gives ultimate meaning to the human existence and should shape our life and praxis as Christ followers.

18

Exegesis

EXEGESIS: "The explanation and exposition of a text, with attention to such matters as determination of text, translation and paraphrase, and interpretation of structure, setting, and purpose."[1]

I'm sure it's apparent by now that I'm a total word nerd, and one of the reasons I like this particular word is its etymology, which refers to how it was "born" and how it evolved as it spread from one language to another. English speakers have used the word *exegesis* to describe the careful, analytical study of biblical passages in order to produce useful interpretations since the early seventeenth century.[2] That is why we tend to associate exegesis with pastors and teachers whose preaching style is based on verse-by-verse exposition and also involves exploring the original sociohistorical context of a passage/book of the Bible and highlighting nuances in the syntax of the original Hebrew, Greek, and Aramaic language it was inscribed in. And while that style of preaching and teaching is cool for critical thinkers and logophiles (word lovers) like me, it

1. *The Eerdmans Bible Dictionary*, ed. Allen C. Myers (Eerdmans, 1987), under "exegesis."
2. Douglas Stuart, "Exegesis," in *Anchor Yale Bible Dictionary*, vol. 2, 682–88; *Merriam-Webster Dictionary*, "exegesis," accessed October 14, 2025, http://www.merriam-webster.com/dictionary/exegesis.

can be both boring and daunting for folks who *don't* find it exhilarating to spend hours on end going down rabbit holes regarding the original meaning of some obscure ancient word.

So here's an approachable, unintimidating factoid about *exegesis*—mind you, we do have to delve into just a teensy bit of Greek to get there, but please hang with me. The Greek preposition *ex* means "out of," and the second half of this word—*egesis* (literally meaning "to lead" or "to guide")—is closely related to the Greek word *gnosis*, which means "knowledge." Therefore, this term doesn't just represent an academic exercise reserved for pastors, theological scholars, and various other smarty-McTarties. Generally speaking, to "exegete" something can simply mean to *draw knowledge out* of it. As a result, the term *exegesis* is now used far outside the realm of biblical interpretation. A recent Google search brought up a movie review in *The New Yorker* where a logophile moonlighting as a film critic used *exegeses* (a plural form of exegesis) to describe the narrator's intent!

In keeping with a more basic, user-friendly application of exegesis, let's pause right now and exegete our week thus far. What life lessons have you gleaned over the past few days? What ideas became more concrete, and what beliefs became further established in your mind and heart as a result of your personal encounters and experiences? Did you encounter someone or experience something that made an idea less concrete or cause you to question one of your previously held beliefs? Perhaps you ate some surprisingly tasty brussels sprouts that were coated in a blackberry balsamic reduction, causing you to rethink your whole aversion to cruciferous vegetables.

More importantly, what fresh knowledge has Holy Spirit revealed to you over the past few days? And what fresh knowledge have you gotten out of your Bible reading this week? Because God's Spirit and God's Word are the two primary means through which He reveals Himself to us. And regardless of whether we've learned to like vegetables that we hated when we were kids, if we're not getting *something out* of our interaction with them that magnifies Jesus's love for us and increases our love for others, then our system of exegesis needs to be recalibrated or replaced!

- **WHY *EXEGESIS* MATTERS:** Because the critical process of carefully understanding the original context and intended meaning of biblical texts takes us beyond simply accruing data about God and His Word—it carries us toward a more imitable understanding of Scripture and more relational intimacy with Jesus. Exegesis requires marinating in this divine love letter we call the Bible—even attempting to perceive and feel what the original audience must have understood and felt. Just imagine how that first-century Jewish crowd responded when Jesus told the compelling story of the compassionate "Dad" running toward his prodigal son, especially in light of how they thought they had to obey six-hundred-plus rules in the Hebrew Scriptures as a prerequisite for a distant relationship with Yahweh. Sure, exegesis takes more time and effort than a cursory reading of Scripture, but the dividends are invaluable—we gain access to so much more joy, hope, peace, comfort, and confidence when we have a clearer picture of who our God is and how very much He loves us.

19

The Filioque Clause

■ **THE FILIOQUE CLAUSE:** An addition to the Nicene Creed made at the Council of Toledo in AD 589.[1] The word *filioque* (pronounced fee-lee-OH-kway) means "and son" in Latin.[2] Therefore, the Filioque Clause clarifies that the Holy Spirit proceeds from both God the Father *and God the Son* rather than solely from God the Father.[3]

Thom Rainer, pastor, author, and the former president of Lifeway, surveyed people on social media about silly disagreements they'd observed in their local church and then published the twenty-five "silliest" reasons for discord in Christian congregations, which I narrowed down to ten to minimize eye-roll injuries:

1. Whether the length of the worship pastor's beard was appropriate
2. Whether to put restroom stall dividers in the women's restroom
3. Whether the worship leader should have his shoes on during the service
4. Whether cran-grape juice could be served during communion instead of just plain grape juice

---

1. Daniel C. Akin, ed., *A Theology for the Church*, rev. ed. (B&H Academic, 2014), 509.
2. Got Questions Ministries, "What Is the Filioque Clause/Filioque Controversy?," in *Got Questions? Bible Questions Answered* (Faithlife, 2002–13), Logos edition.
3. Got Questions Ministries, "What Is the Filioque Clause?"

5. What brand and blend of coffee to serve in the church foyer (some members left over this dispute)
6. Whether church members could bring deviled eggs to the fellowship supper
7. Whether to use the term *potluck* or *pot blessing* for the fellowship supper
8. Whether vanilla syrup could be part of the church coffee station since it had the same appearance as clear liquor
9. Whether to have gluten-free communion bread
10. Whether to have fake plants as pulpit decorations[4]

Despite the absurdity of these actual arguments among Christ followers, some of them were listed as the main reason people walked away from their home church to find another God squad who would be more accommodating to their partialities. Who would've guessed something as seemingly insignificant as the type of coffee beans used to brew the free java served in the church foyer could cause a breach in the family of God? My point here isn't to poke fun at people's unique likes and dislikes—I appreciate diversity in community and think homogeny is overrated—but I do think it would behoove the body of Christ to focus on the major truths that unify us instead of the minor preferences that threaten to divide us.

The Nicene Creed was first adopted in AD 365 as a unifying standard of Christian faith. It was further supplemented at the second gathering of global church leaders, the Council in Constantinople in AD 381, which is why the version of the Nicene Creed modern Christ followers recite is technically called "the Niceno-Constantinopolitan Creed." Then it was modified again at the third international conference of Christian bishops, the Council of Toledo in AD 589, with a seemingly minor tweak, the Filioque Clause. This edit was made to correct what many

4. Paraphrased from Thom S. Rainer, "Twenty Five Silly Things Church Members Fight Over," *Church Answers* (blog), accessed October 14, 2025, https://churchanswers.com/blog/twenty-five-silly-things-church-members-fight-over.

Christian leaders in that era perceived to be an unintentional slight regarding the authority of Jesus, based on these lines, which were added at Constantinople:

> And in the Holy Spirit, the Lord and life-giver, *Who proceeds from the Father,* Who is worshiped and glorified together with the Father and Son, Who spoke through the prophets.[5]

The theological reasoning for including "and Son" after "Who proceeds from the Father" was based on the following New Testament passages, which include both God the Father and God the Son in sending the Holy Spirit as an advocate for Christ followers immediately after Jesus was resurrected and no longer accessible in His incarnate form:

> *And I will ask the Father, and he will give you another advocate to help you and be with you forever— the Spirit of truth.* The world cannot accept him, because it neither sees him nor knows him. But you know him, for he lives with you and will be in you. I will not leave you as orphans; I will come to you.
>
> . . . *But the Advocate, the Holy Spirit, whom the Father will send in my name, will teach you all things and will remind you of everything I have said to you.* (John 14:16–18, 26)

> *When the Advocate comes, whom I will send to you from the Father*—the Spirit of truth who goes out from the Father—he will testify about me. (John 15:26)

> But what does it matter? The important thing is that in every way, whether from false motives or true, Christ is preached. And because of this I rejoice.
>
> Yes, and I will continue to rejoice, for I know that through your prayers and *God's provision of the Spirit of Jesus Christ* what has happened to me will turn out for my deliverance. (Phil. 1:18–19)

5. Leith, *Creeds of the Churches*, 33.

Yet despite what appear to be sound biblical roots, this petite clause—which most modern believers have never even heard of, much less can pronounce—is what ultimately led to the schism between the Roman Catholic Church and the Eastern Orthodox tradition, because leaders in the Eastern Orthodox tradition argued the Filioque Clause undermined the divinity of the Holy Spirit. Furthermore, since leaders of the Protestant Reformation affirmed the "double possession" doctrine of *filioque,* it also created a relational rupture between Protestant Christ followers and Eastern Orthodox Christ followers.

I'm sure our ancestors of faith didn't plan on splintering into so many different factions, but I can't help wondering how much more unified Christ followers could be today if we followed the advice of German theologian Rupertus Meldenius (who may have been paraphrasing Augustine): "In the essentials unity, in non-essentials liberty, and in all things charity."[6] Because when the infinite mystery of God is filtered through the finite minds, pens, and mouths of mere human beings, some things are bound to be misunderstood, distorted, and miscommunicated. If we don't have some measure of grace for our brothers and sisters in Christ, we better start pinching pennies to purchase a private island where we're the only ones who get to write and enforce the rules.

- **WHY *THE FILIOQUE CLAUSE* MATTERS:** Respectful unity among Christ followers is an incredibly valuable trait in our increasingly divided world where people are looking for a safe community to press into. However, a safe community that honors God and others is not synonymous with cultish uniformity where *everybody* has to agree on *everything*. Christian unity *does* allow for differences in worship style, governance, and even biblical interpretation. Therefore, understanding the minor differences in our theological views can help us when it comes to agreeing on the major tenets of our belief system.

6. Dr. Jim Howard and Dr. Don Payne, syllabus and teaching notes, Biblical and Theological Reflection on the Practice of Ministry, Denver Seminary, July 2019.

20

Gnosis

■ **GNOSIS:** This term is derived from the Greek verb *ginosko,* meaning "to know."[1]

In the original Greek language of the New Testament canon, the noun *gnosis* (which means "knowledge") as well as the verb *ginosko* ("to know") are used more than two hundred times. And since most of us use the word *know* (which is a transliterated form of the Greek root word for *gnosis*) in conversation several times a day, we're technically well-versed in that tiny part of the Greek lexicon.

However, *knowing* has a negative spin too, because *gnosticism* is also derived from the word *gnosis.* And Gnosticism is the heretical belief system that emphasizes a dualistic worldview wherein the material and spiritual realms are segregated, as well as "secret" knowledge (gnosis) about God that was reserved for a select few.

Gnostics, whose mythology infiltrated first- and second-century Christian church culture like a virus, considered themselves to be the elite "chosen people." Their hierarchical and heretical belief system included the concept of a "subordinate god," who they believed created the world, and a "higher

1. Wayne A. Detzler, *New Testament Words in Today's Language* (Victor Books, 1986), 252.

god," who ruled over the created world but didn't sully himself with the dirty, physical aspects of it like Jesus did. The goal of this dualistic ideology was that with the help of insight (gnosis), the elect could be freed from the fetters of this world. Because according to them, salvation was a matter not of deliverance from sin and guilt, as in orthodox Christianity, but of the freeing of the spirit from matter—in particular, the material human body.[2]

Although Paul didn't explicitly use the term *Gnosticism* (that term wasn't used until the late 1600s), several of his letters appear to address similar misguided thinking and mysticism that predated Gnosticism, which was ultimately condemned as heresy by the early church. While most Gnostic sects faded away by the end of the sixth century, you can find echoes of Gnosticism in modern belief systems that emphasize some type of faraway, unreachable "creator of the cosmos," extreme segregation between the physical/tangible world and the spiritual/intangible world, and elitism that tends to fall along ethnic and/or socioeconomic lines. Yet somehow these broken belief systems still attract hordes of disciples and sometimes even masquerade as sound doctrine by framing themselves with a few Bible verses. We've got to be more discerning with regard to the books we read, shows we watch, podcasts we listen to, and people we follow on social media. If the content doesn't line up with God's Word, it's *not* wisdom.

I'll never forget a conversation I had with a less-than-wise woman at a church thirty-plus years ago when I first started teaching the Bible vocationally. We were standing in the foyer outside the sanctuary right after the program concluded when she casually approached me and said something along the lines of "Your message on grace—God's unmerited favor—was really good for *them*." At which point she gestured to the rest of the women in attendance, most of whom were still sitting in the sanctuary. Then she added with a whiff of condescension, "I'm so glad I've gotten to the point where I don't need His

2. Kurt Rudolph, "Gnosticism," in *Anchor Yale Bible Dictionary*, vol. 2, 1033–34.

grace anymore." I assumed she was teasing and waited a long beat for the punch line. But instead of making a self-deprecating joke, she went on to explain how she'd climbed to the top of the ladder of spiritual enlightenment. I thought, *Oh, wow, this lady actually* believes *she's matured to some ethereal state of perfection!* And it took a lot of restraint not to take several steps away from her because I didn't want to be zapped by stray electrons when she got struck by lightning. I've thought about that awkward conversation many times in the years since and can't help wondering if that misguided woman's friends and family (assuming she has any) agree with her smug self-assessment.

Because *gnosis* by itself has all too often been distorted into narcissistic beliefs that aren't biblically defensible, the term is sometimes translated as "head knowledge."

- **WHY *GNOSIS* MATTERS:** Instead of leading to humility and gratitude for what God has done for us, gnosis by itself tends to lead to pride, self-elevation, unhealthy individualism, and hierarchical thinking. A mind filled with information about God yet segregated from a heart that's been tendered by His divine grace can make one quite unpleasant, even insufferable! Which is surely why the apostle Paul explained to those young, knowledge-obsessed Greeks in Corinth, "We know that 'We all possess knowledge [gnosis].' But knowledge [gnosis] puffs up while love builds up" (1 Cor. 8:1).

21

Gospel

■ **GOSPEL:** Derived from the Greek word *euangelion* (*yoo-ang-GHEL-ee-on*), which means "good news" or "good tidings." In the context of Christianity, the gospel refers to the message of salvation through Jesus Christ. It encompasses both the historical events of Jesus's life, death, and resurrection and a personal relationship with Him.[1] The term *Gospel* is also used for the first four books of the New Testament, which provide accounts of Jesus's earthly life and ministry. These recorded Gospels, attributed to Matthew, Mark, Luke, and John, were written between AD 60 and 100 and serve as witnesses to Jesus's impact on their authors and the original audiences.[2] The gospel message, preached first by Jesus Christ and then emulated by His disciples and apostles, proclaims the fulfillment of God's plan to save and redeem humanity from the wrath of sin through faith in and devotion to Jesus Christ.

I had my biannual appointment with my dear dermatologist recently, and per usual, I sensed her disappointment over my suntanned skin. I assured

1. Ron Geaves, "Gospel," in *Continuum Glossary of Religious Terms* (Continuum, 2002), 129.
2. Richard R. Melick Jr. and Shera Melick, *Teaching That Transforms* (B&H Academic, 2010), 58.

her for the umpteenth time that I slather myself with prescription sunscreen and wear large hats that shade my face whenever we're at the lake or hiking, biking, playing pickleball, etc. But then I reminded her that I've always been and always will be an outdoorsy kind of girl and therefore will probably never have the vampire routine and porcelain skin she prefers. She was friendly while performing her customary full-body mole-and-suspicious-freckle check, but after hovering over a new brown spot under my collarbone, she explained that she needed to do a small biopsy because it presented like the basal cell carcinomas I've had to have removed in the past. Thankfully, a week later I got a voicemail from her nurse that started with "I've got *good news*, Lisa," after which she explained that it turned out to be just an "age spot"—which frankly sounded more like "rude news" to me because if I develop many more of these mature-skin decorations, surely children will start approaching me with markers, compelled by their urge to connect my dots!

While we tend to associate the word *gospel* solely with Christianity in modernity, this expression of good news was used prior to the earthly ministry of Jesus Christ. Although, among ancient Greeks *euangelion/gospel* referred to the news of a military victory and/or an imperial message, so it carried a bit more gravitas than a harmless mole report. Furthermore, Roman emperors usually had several "gospels" because they were like the State of the Union addresses that presidents in the United States give to advance their policies and inspire the populace. The terms *savior* and *god* were commonplace in the Greco-Roman world long before Jesus was born in Bethlehem too. Instead of referring to the Messiah, *gospel, savior,* and *god* were initially used in reference to whatever human emperor was reigning at that point in time.[3]

The following inscription honoring the first official Roman emperor, Caesar Augustus, dated 9 BC, provides a great example of the divine status given to Roman emperors. Now, for those of you who examined your eyelids through

3. Steven J. Friesen, *Imperial Cults and the Apocalypse of John: Reading Revelation in the Ruins* (Oxford University Press, 2001), 32–36.

most of ancient world history in high school, here's the CliffsNotes: Caesar Augustus was the great-nephew of Julius Caesar, who was the ruthless military commander who set in motion the plans for Rome to be governed by one sole emperor instead of by the relative democracy of the senate. Augustus was later adopted as Julius Caesar's son, and he shrewdly took his dad's surname as his formal first name, thereby coupling him to Julius Caesar's larger-than-life reputation and authority. It's not hard to imagine him preening over this kind of flattery:

> Whereas the providence that ordains our whole life has established with zeal and distinction that which is most perfect in our life by bringing Augustus, who she filled with virtue as a benefaction to all humanity; sending to us and to those after us *a savior* who put an end to war and brought order to all things *the birth of the god* was the beginning of *good tidings* [gospel] to the world through him.[4]

The bottom line of that fancy prose is that Augustus was heralded as "a benefaction to all humanity" and a "savior" to the citizens of Rome because, through his military might, he'd "put an end to war" and therefore brought peace to the world and "order to all things." He's therefore praised as a "god," whose birth was understood as "the beginning of good tidings [aka the gospel] to the world."

All of which not only might sound familiar if you're a Christ follower but also might cause you to start humming a Christmas carol because just look at the similarities in Luke's birth narrative about Jesus:

> And there were shepherds living out in the fields nearby, keeping watch over their flocks at night. An angel of the Lord appeared to them, and the glory of the Lord shone around them, and they were terrified. But the angel said to

4. Wilhelm Dittenberger, ed., *Orientis Graeci Inscriptiones Selectae: Supplementum Sylloges Inscriptionum Graecarum*, vol. 1 (S. Hirzel, 1903), 41–42 (emphasis mine).

> them, "Do not be afraid. *I bring you good news* that will cause great joy for all the people. Today in the town of David a Savior *has been born to you; he is the Messiah,* the Lord. This will be a sign to you: You will find a baby wrapped in cloths and lying in a manger." (Luke 2:8–12)

The parallels in these two announcements are unmistakable, but the "gospels" they're preaching are polar opposites, which is well summarized by Anglican priest and theologian Dr. Matthew Halsted:

> Unlike Caesar's "gospel," which was founded upon war and violence, Jesus' gospel is a gospel of the cross—a gospel of self-giving, enemy-embracing love (1 Cor. 1:17–19; Phil. 2:5–11; Lk. 23:34). Only Jesus brings true "peace" to the earth because he, *through* his cross and resurrection, has "disarmed the rulers and the authorities" and has therefore "overcome the world" (Col. 2:15; Jn. 16:33). As Luke records in his account, all the glory goes to "God in the highest." And, for these early Christians, *that* God was most certainly not Caesar. *Amen.*[5]

The term *gospel* became increasingly associated with Christianity in the New Testament era, as evidenced by how Paul cheekily hijacks the term to describe the infinitely superior *good news* of the life and ministry of Jesus Christ:

> Fellow children of Abraham and you God-fearing Gentiles, it is to us that this message of salvation has been sent. The people of Jerusalem and their rulers did not recognize Jesus, yet in condemning him they fulfilled the words of the prophets that are read every Sabbath. Though they found no proper ground for a death sentence, they asked Pilate to have him executed. When they had carried out all that was written about him, they took him down from the cross and laid him in a tomb. But God raised him from the dead, and for

5. Matthew L. Halsted, "The Gospel of Caesar?," Dr. Matthew L. Halsted, August 10, 2020, https://matthewhalsted.com/2020/08/10/the-gospel-of-caesar (italics in the original).

> many days he was seen by those who had traveled with him from Galilee to Jerusalem. They are now his witnesses to our people.
>
> We tell you *the good news* [euangelion/Gospel]: What God promised our ancestors he has fulfilled for us, their children, by raising up Jesus. (Acts 13:26–33)

The news Paul preached about how Jesus Christ, the Son of God and second member of the Trinity, became like us in order to save us is so much more than "good." It's by far the *best* news humanity has ever received!

- **WHY THE *GOSPEL* MATTERS:** It's the key to how sinners like us can be reconciled into the unconditional love of a Holy God. It's also the supernatural conduit connecting us to Jesus's promise in John 10:10: "I have come that they may have life, and have it to the full." And the *good news* of Jesus Christ provides the essential meaning, purpose, and mission for how we live as God's image bearers here on earth.

22

Grace

GRACE: In theological terms, grace is understood as unmerited favor, with God extending forgiveness and salvation through Jesus Christ to sinful humanity while withholding deserved judgment.[1] The concept of God's unmerited favor is central to the Christian belief system, although there are nuances in understanding and application. The Old Testament presents the redemption of the Hebrew people from Egypt as a supreme example of God's grace, emphasizing that it was not due to Israel's merit but despite their unrighteousness. Ultimately, the grace of God is seen as supremely revealed and given through the person and work of Jesus Christ, who is described as both the beneficiary and the embodiment of God's grace.[2]

Bible scholars and theologians assert that the concept of grace first entered the biblical lexicon in Genesis 6 when Noah was pointed out as the lone bright spot in the wicked blight humanity had become: "But Noah found *favor* in the eyes of the LORD" (Gen. 6:8).

1. Donald K. McKim, *The Westminster Dictionary of Theological Terms*, 2nd ed. (Westminster John Knox, 2014), under "grace."

2. Ronald F. Youngblood, F. F. Bruce, and R. K. Harrison, eds., *Nelson's New Illustrated Bible Dictionary*, rev. and updated ed. (Thomas Nelson, 1995), under "grace."

The Hebrew word *hēn* (not to be confused with a female chicken) is what "favor" is translated from here, but it can also mean "grace, charm, or popularity." And while I'm more of a wannabe than a true academic scholar, I would argue that the *concept* of grace precedes the first mention of the word *hēn*/grace in Genesis 6:8 because, at the very beginning of the story, God lovingly created us in His image—with inherent dignity and value *we hadn't earned* (see Gen. 1:26–27). Then He gave us an antidote for loneliness that *we hadn't earned* (see Gen. 2:18–25). And then—after Eve got deceived by the father of lies, who manipulated her into questioning the very goodness of God—there was even more favor *they didn't deserve*:

> The LORD God made garments of skin for Adam and his wife and clothed them. And the LORD God said, "The man has now become like one of us, knowing good and evil. He must not be allowed to reach out his hand and take also from the tree of life and eat, and live forever." So the LORD God banished him from the Garden of Eden to work the ground from which he had been taken. After he *drove the man out*, he placed on the east side of the Garden of Eden cherubim and a flaming sword flashing back and forth to guard the way to the tree of life. (Gen. 3:21–24)

I don't know about you, but I usually have mental pictures scrolling through my head like a movie when I read biblical narrative because these are true stories and I like to imagine what it might've been like when they happened. In this instance, I used to imagine Eve wearing Daisy Duke cutoff jean shorts, a crop top with a hard rock album cover emblazoned on it, and a long feather clip-on in her hair. No offense to hard rock music fans, but that's the general outfit of all the wild girls I went to high school with, and let's face it, Eve initially presents as the queen of some ancient wild-girl gang! I mean, if she hadn't gone and totally disobeyed God's only rule after getting deceived by that slithery fruit salesman named Lucifer, the world wouldn't be such a hot mess, would it?

So when verse 24 describes God driving them out of the Garden of Eden, I used to think, *Good riddance!* and imagine her reeling out of there all disheveled and unladylike after Yahweh kicks her tail to the curb. That is, until one of my professors at Denver Seminary chose this exact passage as proof that our God is full of grace.

Dr. Jim Howard taught us that the two words *drove out* in Genesis 3:24 come from a single word in the original Hebraic text—*garash*. And the word *garash* is actually used redemptively in Exodus 10:11 and 11:1 when God's people are being driven out of slavery in Egypt in much the same way a shepherd will drive ignorant sheep out of the rock-and-thistle-strewn fields they've grown accustomed to, toward greener pastures where they will not only have much better grazing but will also be safe from predators. (It's also used in a redemptive context in the title of Psalm 34, one of my favorite Old Testament tunes because David sings about shamelessness immediately after drooling in his beard to escape his enemies [see 1 Sam. 21], which would've been not only shameful but also sacrilegious in that era because a Jewish man's beard was symbolic of his relationship with God. In other words, the scaffolding of that psalm is pure grace too.)

Then Dr. Howard pointed out that the holy bouncers in Genesis 3, the cherubim and the flaming sword God had placed at the edge of the garden to prevent Adam and Eve from returning to Eden, were also for their sake. Because if the original Mr. Dumb and Mrs. Dumber had returned to the garden and eaten from the Tree of Life, they would've been forever frozen in their state of separation from God, never being able to experience the perfect shalom and intimacy with Him that He'd designed for them to enjoy. Which means their offspring—all the way down the line to you and me—wouldn't have the chance to be restored into a right relationship with our Creator Redeemer. Contrary to popular belief and most Sunday school lessons, God wasn't being punitive when He *drove* Adam and Eve *out* of Eden; instead, He was ushering them toward the first steps of redemptive history, and the favor He showed them was *utterly unmerited.*

The grace train just keeps on rolling as we turn the pages of this divine love story called the Bible: God grants fertility to an *undeserving* octogenarian couple named Abe and Sarah, then provides a ram instead of receiving their son Isaac as a sacrifice. He reconciles an *undeserving* murderer named Moses to Himself through a flaming topiary and then picks that unlikely fellow to lead His *undeserving* people out of captivity in Egypt. He carves a dry pathway through a literal ocean at the beginning of their trek to Israel, showers them with food from heaven, warms them at night with His abiding fire, and delivers them to the land He'd promised via another supernatural water crossing by parting the Jordan River for their safe passage when it was at flood stage. Yet, throughout most of those forty years of God's provision, protection, and providence, His people were ungrateful, whiny idolaters. They didn't *deserve* manna and miracles. Once again, their survival was due to our Creator Redeemer's *unmerited favor*.

It's pretty much the same song, different tune throughout the rest of the Old Testament because that cycle of rebellion, repentance, and revival just keeps repeating itself. If it weren't for God's amazing grace, the proverbial train of humanity would've careened off the tracks before the first stop! Of course, the theme of unmerited divine favor continues in the New Testament, although grace is now translated from the Greek word *charis*, which is recorded over 150 times, and it has a name—*Jesus*!

Paul's epistles are absolutely riddled with the theme of how grace was embodied in our Messiah's life and ministry and is now available to everyone who puts their faith in Him. He employs the word *charis/grace* over one hundred times and uses it liberally—like a comprehensive menu of God's goodness! For instance, in 2 Corinthians he uses grace as:

- **A greeting:** "*Grace* and peace to you from God our Father and the Lord Jesus Christ" (2 Cor. 1:2).
- **A way to express gratitude:** "He has delivered us from such a deadly peril, and he will deliver us again. On him we have set our hope that

he will continue to deliver us, as you help us by your prayers. Then many will give thanks on our behalf for the *gracious favor* granted us in answer to the prayers of many" (2 Cor. 1:10–11).

- **A divine enabling:** "All this is for your benefit, so that the *grace* that is reaching more and more people may cause thanksgiving to overflow to the glory of God" (2 Cor. 4:15).
- **A means of salvation:** "As God's co-workers we urge you not to receive God's *grace* in vain. For he says, 'In the time of my favor I heard you, and in the day of salvation I helped you.' I tell you, now is the time of God's favor, now is the day of salvation" (2 Cor. 6:1–2).
- **A way to express generosity:** "But since you excel in everything—in faith, in speech, in knowledge, in complete earnestness and in the love we have kindled in you—see that you also excel in this *grace* of giving" (2 Cor. 8:7).

Since the great apostle Paul didn't narrow grace down to a concise definition or single application, I certainly won't attempt to. I will instead close with one of my favorite excerpts on grace outside of Holy Writ:

> Grace makes its appearance in so many forms that I have trouble defining it. I am ready, though, to attempt something like a definition of grace in relation to God. *Grace means there is nothing we can do to make God love us more*—no amount of spiritual calisthenics and renunciations, no amount of knowledge gained from seminaries and divinity schools, no amount of crusading on behalf of righteous causes. *And grace means there is nothing we can do to make God love us less*—no amount of racism or pride or pornography or adultery or even murder. Grace means that God already loves us as much as an infinite God can possibly love.[3]

3. Philip Yancey, *What's So Amazing About Grace?* (Zondervan, 1997), 70 (italics in the original).

- **WHY *GRACE* MATTERS:** Since Scripture makes it clear it is only by God's *grace* that we can be saved through faith in Jesus Christ (see Eph. 2:8–9), it is our lifeline. The miraculous "finger" of God touching Adam in Michelangelo's painting is not mere art; it is a true representation of a perfectly holy and transcendent God who compassionately made a way for sinful humans to be forgiven, reconciled, and adopted into His family forever.

23

Hermeneutics

- **HERMENEUTICS:** Derived from the Greek verb *hermeneuein* (an ancient word that is also linked to the Greek "messenger god" Hermes), which means "to express, explain, translate or interpret."[1] In the most general terms, *hermeneutics* can be described as the "art of understanding." In the context of Christianity, *hermeneutics* refers to the branch of theology that deals with our interpretation of Scripture and the principles of biblical exegesis. So hermeneutics is effectively the lens through which we read, examine, understand, and ultimately apply the sacred, God-breathed—or *theopneustic*—words in our Bibles.

During my early thirties I lived in Colorado Springs and used to really enjoy trail running. My favorite trail was in Palmer Park, not too far from my house, and it wound two and a half miles up through a peaceful evergreen forest until it ended in a beautiful alpine meadow from which there were amazing views of Pikes Peak. I ran up that dirt path and prayed in that meadow more times than I can count during my six years as a Colorado resident. It was one of my favorite places to relax and lean into God's presence, which is why I

1. Mark L. Y. Chan, "Hermeneutics," in *Global Dictionary of Theology: A Resource for the Worldwide Church*, ed. William A. Dyrness and Veli-Matti Kärkkäinen (IVP Academic, 2008), 379.

was disappointed when our local newspapers and TV stations began reporting about violent crimes that had taken place in Palmer Park. The reports included frightening details about several women who'd been attacked while hiking, mountain biking, or trail running by themselves and advised against further activity in the park until the perpetrator (details in each of the incidents were similar, so police thought it was likely the same man) was arrested. However, one weekend soon after hearing those reports, we were blessed with gorgeous weather, and I found myself driving to Palmer Park with the assumption that it was just too pretty for criminal activity that day.

I did notice there was only one other car parked at the trailhead, as well as the new warning signs posted about the recent assaults. But I pushed the seed of apprehension aside and began my usual uphill route at a brisk pace. I cruised through majestic ponderosa pines while singing worship songs and felt my soul sighing contentedly. That is, until I got to the top of the trail, because right before I stepped into that familiar meadow, I noticed a *naked man* on a rustic bench about fifty feet in front of me!

I thought, *Good night, I can't believe this—I've run smack into the criminal in his birthday suit!* Then I realized in a panic just how vulnerable I was. I hadn't seen another hiker, biker, or runner on the trail, so there would be no one to hear me scream for help. I'd also left my cell phone in my car, so I couldn't call the police. Plus, the sun was starting to slide behind the Rocky Mountains, so it was getting darker. My mounting anxiety knocked my level head off-kilter, leaving me only two rational thoughts as I crouched there, trembling, behind a tree, hoping Mr. Nudity wouldn't notice me:

1. Someone told me men who expose themselves are typically cowards and nonconfrontational.
2. I read in a hiking magazine that if you come upon a wild animal in the woods—unless it's a bear—it behooves you to put your hands over your head and slowly advance toward them, all the while making deep

> guttural sounds because that causes the wild animal to view you as a taller and more aggressive critter instead of prey.

Those two deliberations congealed into what seemed rational in the moment, and I hastily decided to confront the criminal before he grabbed me. So I took a deep breath, then leapt out from my hiding place with my hands over my head and ran toward him, yelling, "HEY," in the deepest voice I could manage. I was surprised when my crazy hunch worked and he jumped up and ran in the opposite direction! I was even more surprised when my clean line of sight—which had been partially obscured by the pine tree, the shadows, and my premonitions—revealed that he was wearing shorts. Very small, blue shorts, which had a deep slit up the thigh and splayed open when he sat, giving him the appearance of a naked ne'er-do-well, when in fact he was probably just a regular dude with unfortunate taste in running apparel.

I got so tickled watching him sprint away from me because he kept looking back over his shoulder, obviously worried that I was going to start chasing him. I thought, *I bet that was his car in the parking lot, and when he gets to it, he's going to call the police and say, "It's a GIRL up there terrorizing everybody!"* Poor guy is probably still in therapy, trying to get past his phobia of loud women in the woods.

Scaring innocent men loitering in mountain meadows is mild compared to the damage we can do if our sight of who God reveals Himself to be is blurred. Which is what can happen if we bring faulty hermeneutics to the Holy Scriptures. We must endeavor to view God's Word with a clean lens, without the "smudge" of preferences, premonitions, or preconceived ideas. And while it's not necessary to remember the academic definition of theological terms like *hermeneutics* or *exegesis,* much less how to spell them, it *is* important to wipe the fog off our proverbial glasses before perusing this awesome, authoritative, supernatural love story called the Bible.

That was Peter's point when he wrote this about Paul's epistles: "His letters contain some things that are hard to understand, which ignorant and unstable people distort, as they do the other Scriptures, to their own destruction" (2 Pet. 3:16). In other words, if we aren't careful about how we read, examine, understand, and ultimately apply God's words, this divine love story *can* be distorted. Therefore, it's a good idea for Christ followers to develop the following healthy hermeneutical habits:

- Pray for discernment before diving into God's Word.
- Read His promises and parameters with gratitude and humility.
- Consider the author, original audience, and sociohistorical context of each book of the Bible you're reading/studying.
- Engage in the Holy Scriptures both privately *and* communally. (If you only read the Bible alone, it's like observing a sky filled with shooting stars night after night in isolation—it's beautiful, but after a while you'll find yourself thinking, *It'd sure be nice to have someone to ooh and ahh over this with!*)

■ **WHY *HERMENEUTICS* MATTERS:** Our view of who our Creator Redeemer is can be dangerously fuzzy. We all need the eyes of our hearts to be enlightened (see Eph. 1:18) when it comes to how God reveals Himself through Scripture, lest we imagine monsters and miss the miracles.

24

The Hypostatic Union

■ **THE HYPOSTATIC UNION:** An important Christological distinction that attempts to describe the miraculous bringing together of humanity and divinity in the same person, Jesus Christ, such that He is both fully divine and fully human.[1]

Several months ago, my friend Shannon invited me to an event that I didn't want to attend but that I went to anyway out of respect for her. It's not that I dislike gathering in general; it's just that I was flat worn out and was hoping to enjoy a relaxing night at home in my pajamas, watching a cooking show and cuddling up with a pint of ice cream. Instead, I changed into clean clothes and drove across town with a heavy sigh.

It didn't take long for my spirits to lift while chatting with friends before the program started. By the time it was ending, I wanted to linger! So when Shannon explained that we were going to share a time of prayer before concluding, I thought, *This is like that last bowl of porridge Goldilocks slurped—it just feels right.* She began by asking anyone who was struggling with loneliness to stand, and

1. Stanley Grenz, David Guretzki, and Cherith Fee Nordling, *Pocket Dictionary of Theological Terms*, The IVP Pocket Reference Series (IVP Academic, 1999), under "*hypostasis*, hypostatic union."

when I noticed a woman near me standing, I got up and walked toward her, thinking, *She's already bravely acknowledged being lonely; the least I can do is hug her so she doesn't have to stand there by herself.*

The second I put my arms around her, it was like her emotional dam broke, and she began to sob. I assumed our tender moment would be brief, but the intercessory prayer went on so long that our embrace segued from sweet to a bit awkward. When I pulled my head back to inject some levity into our unplanned fusion, she whispered hoarsely, "I'm sorry." I whispered back, "Oh no, please don't be sorry. I love this kind of authenticity." But she whispered with more fervency, "No, I'm *really* sorry." When I tried to explain again how grateful I was to connect on a deep level, she gently cut me off with the confession, "I'm not sorry about the hug; I'm sorry I got a big glob of snot in your hair!"

Of course, I took a shower when I got home, and when I stepped out with freshly shampooed hair and caught my reflection in the foggy mirror, I smiled. I found myself musing, *I've been to over fifty Christ-centered events this year, and the holiest thing I think I've gotten to experience was standing close enough to another image bearer that I got the residue of her heartache in my hair.* Then I found my heart dumbfounded over the fact that Jesus—the King of all kings—condescended to be close enough to get the residue of our heartache on His hands, His feet, His side, and His head. He's not some faraway deity or an existential construct; He's the second member of the Triune Godhead, and He's closer than our next breath. That is the practical takeaway of the hypostatic union.

The undiluted deity of Jesus Christ is one of the cornerstones of the Christian faith. From the very beginning of the formation of our belief system, the fact that Jesus has a divine nature—that He's really and truly *God* in the flesh—has been nonnegotiable. In fact, the divinity of Jesus was so imperative to orthodoxy that it was the central focus of the first two formal meetings of ancient spiritual leaders at the Council of Nicaea in AD 325 and the Council of Constantinople in AD 381.

Those early church bishops concluded that Jesus the Son's nature was the exact same nature or substance as God the Father's. But you know how it is with mistake-prone Christ followers—we tend to get in one ditch or another. Simply suggest a carpeting color change in the sanctuary and watch the ensuing fireworks! So, about a century after the matter of Jesus's divinity seemed to be conclusively settled, another formal meeting of Christian leaders had to be convened at the Council of Chalcedon in AD 451 to condemn an "overcorrection" that happened after Nicaea and Constantinople, which was the erroneous assumption some were making that since Jesus was fully divine, He couldn't possibly be fully human at the same time.

One ancient leader who held this unorthodox view went so far as to insist that when Jesus cried at the tomb of Lazarus, they were faux tears . . . the tears of an actor![2] Thankfully, the Council of Chalcedon clarified that Jesus Christ has *two* natures and is paradoxically both truly *divine* and truly *human* simultaneously. The theological term for this truism is *hypostasis*, which is the Greek word for "subsistence," although in the patristic era (the first five centuries AD) it was used as a technical term for "person," and in the modern era of medical terminology it also refers to the accumulation of fluid or blood in the lower parts of the body or organs under the influence of gravity, such as in the case of poor circulation. So the singular word *hypostasis* can be a little tricky! That is why the two words, *hypostatic union*, tend to be used to describe the symbiotic relationship between Jesus's divine and human natures, which our forefathers waxed eloquent about in *The Definition of Chalcedon*:

> We, then, following the holy fathers, all with one consent teach men to confess one and the same Son, our Lord Jesus Christ, the same perfect in Godhead and also perfect in manhood; truly God and truly man, of a rational soul and body; coessential with the Father according to the Godhead, and consubstantial with us according to the manhood; in all things like unto us, without sin; begotten before all ages of the Father according to the Godhead,

2. Dr. Don Payne, class lecture notes, Biblical and Theological Reflection on the Practice of Ministry, Denver Seminary, July 2019.

> and in these latter days, for us and for our salvation, born of the Virgin Mary, the mother of God, according to the manhood; one and the same Christ, Son, Lord, Only-begotten, to be acknowledged in two natures, *without confusion, without change, without division, without separation*; the distinction of natures being by no means taken away by the union, but rather the property of each nature being preserved, and concurring in one person and one subsistence, not parted or divided into two persons, but one and the same Son, and only begotten, God the Word, the Lord Jesus Christ; as the prophets from the beginning have declared concerning Him, and the Lord Jesus Christ Himself has taught us, and the creed of the holy fathers has handed down to us.[3]

In other words:

- Jesus is *without confusion,* so He's not an accidental amalgamation like some divine Frankenstein.
- Jesus is *without change,* so He's not a diluted version of His former glory prior to the incarnation.
- Jesus is *without division,* so He's not a fickle part-time God / part-time human who can't make up His mind.
- Jesus is *without separation,* so He's not a fragile union, sure to break up, like the Beatles.

■ **WHY *THE HYPOSTATIC UNION* MATTERS:** The fact that Jesus is the King of all kings and the One who sticks closer than a brother means that He is both perfectly authoritative and perfectly accessible. Our Savior's divinity demands our wondrous obeisance; His humanity invites us into a warm embrace.

3. Bria Burns, "The Unity of Jesus' Person," in *Lexham Survey of Theology,* Logos edition (emphasis mine).

25

Imago Dei

■ **IMAGO DEI:** "Latin expression for 'image of God,' referring particularly to the climax of God's creation when he made humankind in his 'image' (*selem*) and in his 'likeness' (*dĕmût*)."[1]

This theological premise is rooted in Genesis 1:26–27:

> Then God said, *"Let us make mankind in our image, in our likeness,* so that they may rule over the fish in the sea and the birds in the sky, over the livestock and all the wild animals, and over all the creatures that move along the ground."
>
> *So God created mankind in his own image,*
> *in the image of God he created them;*
> *male and female he created them.*

The Latin term *imago Dei* literally means "image of God." This redemptive concept was first preached by Irenaeus, the Bishop of Lyons, in the second century.

Although there has been considerable debate among theologians about the specific application of *imago Dei*, most agree it means all people contain

1. Bill T. Arnold, *Encountering the Book of Genesis* (Baker Academic, 1998), 222.

a diverse collection of godlike qualities that together make up our personhood.[2] And based on the Hebrew preposition *in* of Genesis 1:26–27, the actual image of God isn't somehow carved or superimposed "within" us—it's more like an internal compass. I began to better understand the truism of imago Dei when one of my seminary professors explained that the historical context of this concept goes back to the ancient practice of kings putting statues of themselves in places where they couldn't physically be to represent their reign and authority.[3] In other words, imago Dei is not a "thing" that's implanted in us; it's the very essence of who we are as people of God, and the way we live our lives should remind others of the compassionate authority of King Jesus.

This audacious miracle has rightly become a crucial facet of Christian orthodoxy because it also underscores how every single human being throughout history has been made in God's image and is therefore inherently valuable and deserving of dignity. In other words, we weren't made to be missed and marginalized, beaten and brutalized, or violated and victimized. We were created to enjoy a vibrant, intimate relationship with God as well as vibrant, intimate relationships with each other, which together make up the *abundant life* Jesus promised His followers in John 10.

Unfortunately, none of us have been loved *perfectly* by other humans because we're all sinners. Worse still, many of us carry scars due to the abusive behavior of others. Quite frankly, I think much of the angry rhetoric prevalent in modern culture is a reflection of old wounds. People are just flat sick and tired of putting up with exploitation, manipulation, and degradation, whether it came from personal abuse like abandonment and sexual molestation or systemic abuse like misogyny and racism.

---

2. Roger E. Olson, *The Mosaic of Christian Belief: Twenty Centuries of Unity and Diversity*, 2nd ed. (IVP Academic, 2016), 220.

3. Jim Howard and Donald Payne, syllabus and teaching notes, Biblical and Theological Reflection on the Practice of Ministry, Denver Seminary, July 2019.

I read an article not long ago that was written by a lovely woman I used to know from ministry circles. In it, she explained how being deeply hurt and deceived by other Christians had compelled her to spend several years deconstructing Scripture, and she no longer believes the Bible can be read with certainty, nor does she believe that faith in Jesus Christ is the only way through which humans can be restored to a holy God. Reading her deconstruction narrative grieved me because the main cause of her apostasy was the cruelty of other Christ followers. When we don't recognize the inherent value of *every human* we have the distinct privilege of rubbing shoulders with, the tragic result can be rupture instead of revival.

Even though I've been in church since I was in utero and became a follower of Jesus Christ when I was in kindergarten, it took decades longer for me to believe I had any inherent dignity. I began encouraging people to base their identity in the immutable, unconditional love of God long before I could do the same thing myself. Frankly, I think *imago Dei* became one of my favorite theological tenets to ponder and preach because I'm still working on internalizing what I can conceptualize—my slow-to-grasp heart needs to hear it repeated in order to memorize the melody.

Consequently, one of the passages I have on a carousel in my mind is Psalm 139:1–17 because it's an epic ode to the immeasurable worth God ascribed to us before we were even born. If *imago Dei* had a theme song, surely it would be this:

> You have searched me, LORD,
>   and you know me.
> You know when I sit and when I rise;
>   you perceive my thoughts from afar.
> You discern my going out and my lying down;
>   you are familiar with all my ways.
> Before a word is on my tongue
>   you, LORD, know it completely.
> You hem me in behind and before,
>   and you lay your hand upon me.

> Such knowledge is too wonderful for me,
>   too lofty for me to attain.
>
> Where can I go from your Spirit?
>   Where can I flee from your presence?
> If I go up to the heavens, you are there;
>   if I make my bed in the depths, you are there.
> If I rise on the wings of the dawn,
>   if I settle on the far side of the sea,
> even there your hand will guide me,
>   your right hand will hold me fast.
> If I say, "Surely the darkness will hide me
>   and the light become night around me,"
> even the darkness will not be dark to you;
>   the night will shine like the day,
>   for darkness is as light to you.
>
> For you created my inmost being;
>   you knit me together in my mother's womb.
> I praise you because I am fearfully and wonderfully made;
>   your works are wonderful,
>   I know that full well.
> My frame was not hidden from you
>   when I was made in the secret place,
>   when I was woven together in the depths of the earth.
> Your eyes saw my unformed body;
>   all the days ordained for me were written in your book
>   before one of them came to be.
> How precious to me are your thoughts, God!
>   How vast is the sum of them!

What a glorious concept to ponder, that God knows us completely *and* loves us unconditionally.

- **WHY *IMAGO DEI* MATTERS:** *Imago Dei* is the fundamental biblical truth that separates (and elevates) humans from all other created things—from centipedes to comets—and establishes the unique dignity and sanctity of every single human life. In other words, regardless of gender, ethnicity, or creed, all human beings are created in God's image and have inherent, inestimable value.

26

Jesus

■ **JESUS:** The name "Jesus," one of the most common in first-century Palestine, can be transliterated

> *Yeshua* from both Hebrew and Aramaic and is written as *Iesous* in the Greek New Testament. In the Hebrew Bible, *Yeshua* (or *Yehoshua*) is often translated "Joshua," as in the case of Moses' protégé Joshua Son of Nun. The name is a combination of *Ja* or *Ya*, short for *Yahweh* (the Old Testament name for Israel's God; Exod. 3:14), and the Hebrew verb *yasha*, meaning "to save" or "to help." Hence, *Yeshua/Jesus* means "Yahweh/God saves."[1]

When I was a teenager (before cell phones, self-driving cars, or the Internet were invented, when you could find piles of fresh dinosaur bones around every corner), Mom confessed that my name, Lisa, was more of a knee-jerk reaction than a preplanned blessing. She explained that her labor contractions with me had come early and increased in intensity very quickly. In the surprising and painful blur of my birth, she and Dad forgot to pick out a name. So after my bigheaded self (I have a large noggin, but because Mom always assured me its girth was due to the extra-large size of my brain, I never developed an

1. Justin Stratis, "Jesus' Personal Names," in *Lexham Survey of Theology*, Logos edition.

insecurity about it; however, it's hard to find hats that fit, and sometimes it's daunting to force it through the tight neckhole of a new sweater) had been delivered and spanked and the nurse leaned over to ask Mom what she and Dad had decided to call their new daughter, her mind went blank. She said the only name she could think of was from a birth announcement she'd received a month or so previously from a distant relative in Mississippi who'd named her baby girl Lisa Dianne. So that's what they wrote on my birth certificate.

When she told me she'd briefly considered naming me Summer since my due date was in late August, it only added insult to the injury of being saddled with Lisa, *the most common female name for girls born in the sixties*[2] (thanks a lot, Elvis). Summer sounds much more exotic, doesn't it? If you called for Lisa over the intercom in a crowded grocery store, gobs of middle-aged women would likely come galloping to the customer service desk. Of course, there are much worse things than having an unexceptional name—Mom could've christened me after one of her pregnancy cravings like "Cheeseburger Extra Onions" or "Chocolate-Dipped Conehead"—but every now and then, I still get wistful about what it might feel like to have someone wave at me from a distance and holler, "Hey, Summer, how ya doing?"

I wonder if Mary found it curious that Angel Gabe told her to name the Son of God she was going to give birth to Jesus (see Luke 1:31), because that name was about as common in first-century Jewish circles as Lisa was in American suburbia in the 1960s. The reason was that God's people had longed for a savior for *centuries*—it was the dominant theme throughout Israel's history and perhaps even more so during periods of persecution, like the Roman oppression that framed the earthly life and ministry of Jesus Christ. Therefore, lots of Jewish mamas named their baby boys Joshua or Hosea (which are English transliterations of the Hebrew name Yeshua, meaning "Yahweh is my salvation") during that era.

2. Macie Reynolds, "The Most Popular Baby Names from the 1960s That Are So Far Out," The Pioneer Woman, September 6, 2024, https://www.thepioneerwoman.com/just-for-fun/a62006242/1960s-baby-names/.

Surely, there were several other boys named Jesus in our Messiah's hometown, but He was the only one whose name was prophetic. Because "this Jesus"—as Peter refers to Him in dramatic fashion immediately after Holy Spirit has gotten their Pentecost/post-resurrection party started with divine pyrotechnics—had come to *fulfill* the prophecies:

> Fellow Israelites, I can tell you confidently that the patriarch David died and was buried, and his tomb is here to this day. But he was a prophet and knew that God had promised him on oath that he would place one of his descendants on his throne. Seeing what was to come, he spoke of the resurrection of the Messiah, that he was not abandoned to the realm of the dead, nor did his body see decay. God has raised this Jesus to life, and we are all witnesses of it. Exalted to the right hand of God, he has received from the Father the promised Holy Spirit and has poured out what you now see and hear. For David did not ascend to heaven, and yet he said,
>
> "The Lord said to my Lord:
> Sit at my right hand
> until I make your enemies
> a footstool for your feet." (Acts 2:29–35)

This excerpt from the first of two "Petrine speeches" (the formal title of Peter's duo of sermons recorded in the book of Acts, which helped build the foundation and fan the flames of the early Christian church) is packed full of amazing theology and reaches a Christological crescendo at the end:

> Therefore let all Israel be assured of this: God has made *this Jesus,* whom you crucified, *both Lord and Messiah.* (v. 36)

Just in case anybody missed it when he accused his fellow Israelites of murdering the Messiah earlier in his message (v. 23), Peter bellows it even louder the second time. Then flanking the homicide indictment is this miraculous word coupling that inspired the beginning of the Apostles' Creed: *this Jesus* . . . who is *both Lord and Messiah.*

Before this moment in redemptive history, "Lord" had been a title exclusively ascribed by the Israelites to Yahweh, the God of Israel, and "Messiah" (rendered "Christ" in some English Bible translations) was a title used exclusively to describe the coming Messiah, or the "Anointed One." So Peter's assertion that *this Jesus, from Nazareth* (not only was Jesus a common name but the town He was from was a small rural village of fewer than five hundred people in the Galilean region, the unimpressive "country cousin" of a bustling urban mecca like Jerusalem, which also had bragging rights to "God's house," the temple) was the Savior Yahweh had promised was an audacious claim! And yet the Holy Spirit permeated Peter's words with so much power, conviction, and authority that three thousand people repented and put their hope in *this Jesus* that day:

> When the people heard this, they were cut to the heart and said to Peter and the other apostles, "Brothers, what shall we do?"
>
> Peter replied, "Repent and be baptized, every one of you, in the name of Jesus Christ for the forgiveness of your sins. And you will receive the gift of the Holy Spirit. The promise is for you and your children and for all who are far off—for all whom the Lord our God will call."
>
> With many other words he warned them; and he pleaded with them, "Save yourselves from this corrupt generation." Those who accepted his message were baptized, and about *three thousand were added to their number that day.* (Acts 2:37–41)

And according to Paul, one day a whole lot more folks are going to be triggered into a similar transformation simply based on *the name* of our Redeemer!

> And being found in appearance as a man,
> he humbled himself
> by becoming obedient to death—
> even death on a cross!

> Therefore God exalted him to the highest place
> and gave him the name that is above every name,
> that *at the name of Jesus every knee should bow,*
> in heaven and on earth and under the earth,
> and *every tongue acknowledge that Jesus Christ is Lord,*
> to the glory of God the Father. (Phil. 2:8–11)

■ **WHY *JESUS* MATTERS:** Paul explains it best in Philippians 2, but just to reiterate:

> And he humbled himself even further, going so far as actually to die a criminal's death on a cross. Yet it was because of this that *God raised him up to the heights of heaven and gave him a name which is above every other name, that at the name of Jesus every knee shall bow in heaven and on earth and under the earth, and every tongue shall confess that Jesus Christ is Lord, to the glory of God the Father*. (Phil. 2:8–11 TLB)

27

Katapatic Theology

■ **KATAPHATIC THEOLOGY:** *Kataphatic* (which can also be spelled "cataphatic") is derived from the Greek word *kataphasis*, which means "affirmation." Therefore, kataphatic theology refers to the practice of describing God through positive statements and symbols, which contrasts with apophatic theology.

In the modern Western world, Christian thought and praxis often reveal a kataphatic theme wherein we describe God in knowable terms like, "We hiked to the top of a mountain today, and when we got there and saw all the vibrant flowers blooming, we began spontaneously singing 'Amazing Grace' because His handiwork was just unmistakable!" Kataphatic theology also relies heavily on religious symbolism to connect with God, which is a common practice dating all the way back to the beginning of redemptive history when Noah built an altar as a tangible place to praise God for rescuing him and his family from the flood (see Gen. 8:20) or when Jacob set up a stone pillar at Bethel after he dreamed about a ladder that reached heaven (see Gen. 28:18–19) or when Samuel erected a stone to memorialize how God had given the Israelites victory over the Philistines (see 1 Sam. 7:12; the place the Israelites camped before the battle was Ebenezer [see 1 Sam. 4:1]—which means "stone of help"—and that is why in the biblical context, memorial stones are often referred to as "Ebenezers").

In the New Testament, God's people continued to use evocative language and tangible symbols to memorialize His faithfulness and hang on to theirs. Twice a day, they continued to pray the Shema—which is Israel's confession of faith by which they acknowledge the one true God and His commandments for them based on Deuteronomy 6:4–5: "Hear, O Israel: The LORD our God, the LORD is one. Love the LORD your God with all your heart and with all your soul and with all your strength." As a matter of fact, when that uppity attorney with an agenda asked Jesus the question about the "greatest commandment," Jesus answered by quoting the Shema (see Mark 12:29) before telling the parable of the Good Samaritan. Jesus also refers to several tangible symbols in Matthew 23:5: "Everything they do is done for people to see: They make their phylacteries wide and the tassels on their garments long."

- Phylacteries were strips of parchment—or wooden boxes containing the parchment—that the Pharisees wore on their foreheads and their hands, and sometimes on their left arms, in order to place them close to their hearts in light of His command in Deuteronomy 11:18: "Fix these words of mine in your hearts and minds; tie them as symbols on your hands and bind them on your foreheads." These wearable "prayer boxes" commemorated God's command to love Him with all their heart, soul, and strength (Deut. 6:4–5; see also Exod. 13:3–16).
- The long tassels Jesus refers to in Matthew 23 were worn by the Pharisees in adherence to Numbers 15:37–40, a passage in which God commanded Israelite men to wear tassels with blue cords on the corners of their robes—again with the intent of encouraging them to remember His commands and obey Him.[1]

1. J. Julius Scott Jr., *Jewish Backgrounds of the New Testament* (Baker Academic, 1995), 251–52.

But the Pharisees missed the point and became preoccupied with using symbols to *look* more spiritual instead of *love* God more. They became consumed with who could strap the biggest, fanciest box on their forehead and who could make their fringe super long and noticeable. The symbols that were supposed to direct their attention to God instead captured their attention and morphed into idols.

The same thing happened when Christians in the early church collected "relics"—which were small pieces of bone or the teeth—from religious leaders like Peter, Paul, or a Catholic saint because they thought that owning a tiny, tangible "piece" of someone who'd been close to God somehow made them closer to Him as well. When John of the Cross died in 1592, bystanders basically tore his body apart in order to get a "holy relic." And while the practice of fighting over somebody's teeth probably sounds weird to our modern ears (especially if your stream of the faith is Protestant), it's effectively the same sentiment that drives people to spend outlandish sums nowadays on items that belonged to someone famous, like Elvis, when they're put up for auction. As if owning a blue suede shoe magically makes you a friend of the king of rock and roll.

That is, of course, the inherent danger of purely kataphatic theology. God's people are still prone to become so enamored with evocative worship tunes, trendy Christian apparel, and crucifix-themed jewelry that we forget Who they represent. Sometimes the supernatural nature of our Creator Redeemer can't be captured in a song, by a bracelet, or through a slogan on a T-shirt. Sometimes what we *don't know* about God can compel our knees to bend and our hearts to worship as much as what we *do know*.

■ **WHY *KATAPHATIC THEOLOGY* MATTERS:** It provides a meaningful way for us to engage with and understand some measure of who God is, despite the finite capacity of our human minds. Kataphatic theology is the means through which we, as created beings, can seek to know and understand all we possibly can about our Creator Redeemer. Healthy kataphatic theology acknowledges that while the one true God is not completely knowable or understandable this side of Glory, because of His gracious accommodation to those who seek Him we can know and understand Him in *part* (see 1 Cor. 13:12) through the divine revelation of His Word and Holy Spirit.

28

Kenosis

■ **KENOSIS:** The Greek word *kenosis*, meaning "emptying," refers to Christ's self-emptying or renunciation of certain divine attributes in the incarnation.[1] In Christian theology, kenosis is understood as Christ's voluntary act of humbling Himself by taking on human nature and its limitations while still retaining His divine nature. Some interpretations suggest that Christ veiled or set aside certain divine attributes, such as omniscience and omnipotence, during His earthly ministry. However, it's important to note that kenosis does not imply that Christ ceased to be God, but rather that He added a human nature to His divine nature.[2]

There were so many firsts when I brought Missy home from Haiti after our two-year adoption journey. Her first bubble bath. Her first time watching *Frozen*. Her first Easter egg hunt (she came home the week of Easter). Her first plane ride. Her first escalator ride. Her first elevator ride. Her first hayride. Her first time staying in a hotel. Then, about two weeks after she became an American citizen, I found myself sitting across from her in the sticky booth

1. P. H. Brazier, *C. S. Lewis—An Annotated Bibliography and Resource*, book 4 of C. S. Lewis: Revelation and the Christ (Pickwick, 2012), 150.
2. Got Questions Ministries, "What Is the Kenosis?"

of a fast-food restaurant watching her enthusiastically gobble her first fistful of trans fat–laden fried potatoes. Of course, I'd planned to harvest most of the food we ate from our large garden and the small flock of chickens I'd accrued during the adoption process to make sure Missy's nutrition was as healthy as possible, especially in light of the fact that she'd been malnourished for the better part of the first four years of her precious little life. Unfortunately, my best-laid homesteading plans were bulldozed by the weary-to-the-bone exhaustion of new parenthood.

After happily polishing off her first kids' meal, Missy gestured to the play area and asked hopefully, "Iz it?" which was her universal question for "What is that?" or "May I try that?" or "Will you please take me there?" before she learned to speak English. Since I'd already significantly lowered the health bar for my miracle child, I nodded my head and led her to a square room flanked by glass walls (to magnify the heat of the sun's rays), high ceilings (to accommodate a large, ketchup-smeared slide), and indoor/outdoor carpeting that smelled faintly of urine. There was also a pit filled with thousands of brightly colored plastic balls and three screaming toddlers. Before I could warn her about how flesh-eating bacteria love to lurk in ball pits, my darling daughter hurled herself into the undulating nightmare.

It took her a second to bob to the surface, but when she did, her expression was sheer panic. And before a thought had time to race through my new-mama mind, I'd launched myself into that hellish hole to rescue my baby girl. In the years since I carried Missy out of that restaurant with the manager's stern look of disapproval burning into my back, I've instinctively leapt/crawled/lowered myself into several other dicey scenarios to protect my daughter. Once I even squashed my claustrophobic self into a child-sized playground tube to retrieve her when she got overwhelmed and was afraid to crawl out to the other side! And my love for Missy is a mere drop in the ocean compared to our Savior's love for us, which is where *kenosis* comes in. Jesus willingly "squashed" His deity into the narrow tube of humanity to rescue ragamuffins like us:

> Therefore if you have any encouragement from being united with Christ, if any comfort from his love, if any common sharing in the Spirit, if any tenderness and compassion, then make my joy complete by being like-minded, having the same love, being one in spirit and of one mind. Do nothing out of selfish ambition or vain conceit. Rather, in humility value others above yourselves, not looking to your own interests but each of you to the interests of the others.
>
> In your relationships with one another, have the same mindset as Christ Jesus:
>
> Who, being in very nature God,
> did not consider equality with God something to be used to his own advantage;
> rather, he *made himself nothing* [kenoō—the root of kenosis, to "empty" oneself]
> by taking the very nature of a servant,
> being made in human likeness.
> And being found in appearance as a man,
> he humbled himself
> by becoming obedient to death—
> even death on a cross!
>
> Therefore God exalted him to the highest place
> and gave him the name that is above every name,
> that at the name of Jesus every knee should bow,
> in heaven and on earth and under the earth,
> and every tongue acknowledge that Jesus Christ is Lord,
> to the glory of God the Father. (Phil. 2:1–11)

When we peruse passages like Philippians 2:1–11, which describes Jesus as making himself nothing, or John 13:1–17, which describes Jesus as washing His disciples' feet, or 2 Corinthians 8:9, which describes Jesus as becoming poor, it's imperative to note that He did not in any way forfeit His deity. When our Savior condescended to earth, wrapped in the smooth olive skin of a Jewish baby boy whose first cradle was a rough-hewn feeding trough, He was still wholly and completely divine. The same God who spoke the universe into being also cried for His mother's milk—which is mind-blowing, isn't it? After wielding a scepter in Glory, Jesus chose to squat down and pick up a towel to wash our nasty feet . . . Makes a mom hurling herself into a tee-tee-tainted ball pit completely mild by comparison.

The mind-blowing miracle of kenosis is also evident in the healing encounter Jesus had with a woman who'd been bleeding for twelve years:

> A large crowd followed and pressed around him. And a woman was there who had been subject to bleeding for twelve years. She had suffered a great deal under the care of many doctors and had spent all she had, yet instead of getting better she grew worse. When she heard about Jesus, she came up behind him in the crowd and touched his cloak, because she thought, "If I just touch his clothes, I will be healed." Immediately her bleeding stopped and she felt in her body that she was freed from her suffering.
>
> *At once Jesus realized that power had gone out from him. He turned around in the crowd and asked, "Who touched my clothes?"*
>
> "You see the people crowding against you," his disciples answered, "and yet you can ask, 'Who touched me?'"
>
> *But Jesus kept looking around to see who had done it.* Then the woman, knowing what had happened to her, came and fell at his feet and, trembling with fear, told him the whole truth. He said to her, "Daughter, your faith has healed you. Go in peace and be freed from your suffering." (Mark 5:24–34)

When Jesus asked who touched Him, He wasn't pretending He didn't know who touched Him for dramatic effect. The Old Testament explains that God *can't* lie (see Num. 23:19). Therefore, the only theological explanation that can be reconciled with what Scripture reveals about the perfect character of our Creator Redeemer is that our Savior intentionally "emptied" His omniscience in this situation. Because even though her hemorrhage ceased the second she touched His robe, surely her heart and mind were still riddled with the wounds of being ostracized for over a decade (according to Mosaic law, her bleeding condition made her ceremonially unclean, which meant she wasn't allowed to touch, be touched, or go to temple). But after Jesus compelled her to reveal her identity, she was able to share her story and be fully restored into the family of faith as a *daughter*. He made Himself *less* out of *love*.

- **WHY *KENOSIS* MATTERS:** It offers startling proof of the supernatural lengths our Savior went to in order to redeem us. He condescended to the limits of incarnation out of compassion. He humbled Himself, taking on the very nature of a servant, ultimately submitting to the public degradation of death on a cross because of His unconditional love for us. He became like us—albeit without sin—to save us!

29

Kerygma

■ **KERYGMA:** Related to the Greek noun *kēryx*, which means "proclaimer," and the Greek verb *kēryssō*, which means "to proclaim."[1] Therefore, the theological term *kerygma* typically refers to the verbal proclamation of the gospel, and—depending on the context—it may refer to the content proclaimed or the act of proclaiming.[2]

By all accounts, Florrie Evans was a quiet, unassuming young woman from the village of New Quay, Cardiganshire, in Wales. (FYI: The word *cardigan* came from a fellow who grew up in this town too—Lord Cardiganshire. Evidently, he was a tad claustrophobic, so when he felt trapped in his long-sleeved wool military sweater, he sliced it from top to bottom in the front with his sword, thereby creating the first open-front sweater, which was named after him.) One Sunday in January 1904, the minister of Tabernacle Calvinist Methodist Church, Joseph Jenkins, invited young people to a meeting after the worship service to connect with each other and share their testimonies. During the

1. Douglas Mangum and E. Tod Twist, *2 Timothy*, ed. Douglas Mangum and Derek R. Brown, Lexham Research Commentaries (Lexham Press, 2013), Logos edition.

2. Hobert K. Farrell, "Kerygma," in *Evangelical Dictionary of Biblical Theology*, electronic ed., Baker Reference Library (Baker, 1996), 444.

gathering, Florrie felt compelled to stand up and declare, "I love the Lord Jesus with all my heart!" Historians point to her passionate proclamation as the catalyst of the Welsh revival of 1904–5, which swept through the country, prompting spiritual renewal among Christ followers and during which well over 100,000 people put their hope in Jesus, and the attention of their nation turned toward God.[3]

The word *kerygma* is found eight times in the original Greek text of the New Testament (Matt. 12:41; Luke 11:32; Rom. 16:25–27; 1 Cor. 1:21; 2:4; 15:14; 2 Tim. 4:17; Titus 1:3), and in every case it emphasizes a Florrie-type verbal proclamation, as clearly evidenced in Paul's letter to Christians in Rome:

> Now to him who is able to establish you in accordance with my gospel, *the message I proclaim about Jesus Christ*, in keeping with the revelation of the mystery hidden for long ages past, but now revealed and made known through the prophetic writings by the command of the eternal God, so that all the Gentiles might come to the obedience that comes from faith—to the only wise God be glory forever through Jesus Christ! Amen. (Rom. 16:25–27)

And while the specific word *kerygma* isn't found in the Old Testament (because it's a Greek term!), the same theme of preaching sermons and telling stories—*proclaiming* the mercy and faithfulness of God—echoes throughout. One of my favorites takes place after God dries up the Jordan River—marking His people's entrance into the Promised Land and signaling the end of their forty-year wilderness wandering. He commands Joshua to take twelve stones from the middle of that miraculously dry riverbed and form them into a ceremonial pile. Then He explains that when their children ask them about that fancy stone memorial in the future, they're to proclaim how He cut a path through the Jordan River (just as He had the Red Sea) to rescue and redeem them from captivity and calamity:

3. "Welsh Revival 1904–5," Church Growth Modelling, accessed October 15, 2025, https://churchmodel.org.uk/revival/welsh-revival-1904-5/.

> So when the people broke camp to cross the Jordan, the priests carrying the ark of the covenant went ahead of them. Now the Jordan is at flood stage all during harvest. Yet as soon as the priests who carried the ark reached the Jordan and their feet touched the water's edge, the water from upstream stopped flowing. It piled up in a heap a great distance away, at a town called Adam in the vicinity of Zarethan, while the water flowing down to the Sea of the Arabah (that is, the Dead Sea) was completely cut off. So the people crossed over opposite Jericho. The priests who carried the ark of the covenant of the LORD stopped in the middle of the Jordan and stood on dry ground, while all Israel passed by until the whole nation had completed the crossing on dry ground. . . .
>
> When the whole nation had finished crossing the Jordan, the LORD said to Joshua, "Choose twelve men from among the people, one from each tribe, and tell them to take up twelve stones from the middle of the Jordan, from right where the priests are standing, and carry them over with you and put them down at the place where you stay tonight."
>
> So Joshua called together the twelve men he had appointed from the Israelites, one from each tribe, and said to them, "Go over before the ark of the LORD your God into the middle of the Jordan. Each of you is to take up a stone on his shoulder, according to the number of the tribes of the Israelites, to serve as a sign among you. In the future, when your children ask you, 'What do these stones mean?' *tell them* that the flow of the Jordan was cut off before the ark of the covenant of the LORD. When it crossed the Jordan, the waters of the Jordan were cut off. These stones are to be a memorial to the people of Israel forever." (Josh. 3:14–17; 4:1–7)

I've often heard the sentiment, "Preach the gospel at all times, and when necessary, use words." And since it was usually attributed to Saint Augustine—one of my favorite long-dead pretend theological boyfriends—I used to think it sounded cool and carried weight. It wasn't until I entered the doctoral program at Denver Seminary in my late fifties that I found out Augustine never spoke or wrote those words, which prompted me to ponder the saying. And I found myself thinking, *Hmm, my local barista is nice, but neither his kind demeanor nor the extra dollop of whipped cream he puts on my mocha clarifies who Jesus is or fertilizes my faith in Him. Those Girl Scouts I bought cookies from in front of Target were friendly, but neither their perky salesmanship nor the Thin Mints they talked me into clarified who Jesus is or fertilized my faith in Him. The electrician who hung new ceiling fans in our house was polite and courteous, but even the fact that he swept up after himself didn't clarify who Jesus is or fertilize my faith in Him.* I came to realize that without words—spoken, written, or signed for our hearing-impaired friends and neighbors—the gospel can only be implied at best.

- **WHY *KERYGMA* MATTERS:** Near the end of this redemptive love story we call the Bible, there's a galvanizing glimpse of heaven where God promises the evil dragon named Satan—who is the enemy of our souls and father of lies—is going to be defeated once and for all by the word of our testimony and the blood of God's only begotten Son, Jesus (see Rev. 12:11). And testimonies have to be *told*. Our proclamations about God's goodness and faithfulness are effective tools for evangelism and eschatology.

30

Koinonia

KOINONIA: (pronounced kȯinə'nēə[1] or, phonetically, koy-**now**-knee-uh) A Greek term used in the New Testament that carries multiple meanings related to Christian fellowship and communion. It is often translated as "fellowship," "partnership," "participation," or "sharing." In the New Testament, koinonia describes the close association and participation among believers in the Christian community, centered around common interests, spending time together, and sharing resources.[2]

Around AD 400, a sixteen-year-old boy named Patrick living in what is now known as the northeast coast of England was kidnapped by Celtic pirates who scaled the cliffs of his village in the middle of the night to take young men hostage so they could sell them as slaves back in Ireland. He was eventually bought by a wealthy tribal chief who put him to work herding cattle. While he was enslaved in Ireland, he turned toward God, as he explained in his own words:

1. *Merriam-Webster Dictionary,* "koinonia," accessed October 15, 2025, https://www.merriam-webster.com/dictionary/koinonia.

2. John D. Barry et al., *Faithlife Study Bible* (Lexham Press, 2012, 2016), Logos edition.

> After I had arrived in Ireland, I found myself pasturing flocks daily, and I prayed a number of times each day. More and more the love and fear of God came to me, and faith grew and my spirit was exercised, until I was praying up to a hundred times every day and in the night nearly as often.[3]

Six years after being trafficked, Patrick heard a voice in a dream that instructed him to wake up and walk to the sea, where he'd find a ship waiting to take him back home. So the following morning he slipped away from his captors, walked for several days, found the ship, talked the sailors into letting him on board, and ultimately returned home to England. He then felt compelled to train for the priesthood and, after finishing his religious studies, was ordained as a bishop. Patrick—by then a respected priest—could've spent the rest of his life in the comfort of home, safely ensconced in an English parish. Instead, he sensed God calling him back to Ireland, to the land of his oppressors.

His compassion for the Irish was both remarkable and rare among his peers since the Celts were viewed as barbarians because they were largely illiterate, known to strip naked in battle and howl at the top of their lungs, and often decapitated their enemies. Therefore, Patrick's mission to bring the gospel of Jesus Christ to Ireland was unprecedented and considered foolhardy by most. I mean, goodness gracious, sharing the gospel is one thing, but sharing it with naked hellions is quite another!

Yet, instead of being rebuffed or beheaded, Patrick was embraced by his former captors because he spoke their language, engaged them in conversation, told colorful stories, sang Irish ballads, prayed for the sick, mediated conflicts, and on at least one occasion blessed a river so the fishermen could catch more fish! During his twenty-eight years in Ireland, Patrick baptized thousands of Christian converts, planted approximately seven hundred churches, and was likely the first European leader to denounce slavery in that part of the world.

3. George Hunter, *The Celtic Way of Evangelism: How Christianity Can Reach the West—Again* (Abingdon Press, 2010), 2.

His passion for Christ and his passion for the Irish and their way of life changed the trajectory of the entire nation. In Ireland today, more than six thousand places contain the grammatical element *cill,* which is the ancient Gaelic word for "church"[4] and a testament to Patrick's transformative influence.

Despite those accomplishments, the Catholic church has never canonized Patrick as a saint because he ruffled too many ancient feathers when he steadfastly refused the church's repeated orders to force his parishioners to change their way of life and adopt more formal Roman standards regarding how they dressed, styled their hair, and worshiped. In short, the religious leaders in Rome wanted Irish believers to tone down their zest for life and behave in a more "civilized" manner. But since those rowdy Irish Christians had become his dearest friends and closest companions, Patrick chose to defend their way of life instead of advancing his career. I sure would love to see that jolly old saint's expression on March 17 (the date of his death) when millions of people around the world celebrate St. Patrick's Day, despite the stiff upper lips of his long-dead superiors!

Every time I read the word *koinonia* in a Bible study or commentary, my "sanctified imagination" (we have C. S. Lewis to thank for that wonderful term!) sees it in green because of Pat! *Koinonia* is found in forty-plus verses in the New Testament (there's some variance according to what translation you're reading), and the first time it occurs is in reference to a group of Christ followers who began gathering soon after Peter preached at Pentecost:

> *They devoted themselves to the apostles' teaching and to fellowship,* to the breaking of bread and to prayer. Everyone was filled with awe at the many wonders and signs performed by the apostles. All the believers were together and had everything in common. They sold property and possessions to give to anyone who had need. Every day they continued to meet together in the temple courts. They broke bread in their homes and ate together with glad

4. Hunter, *Celtic Way of Evangelism,* 14.

> and sincere hearts, praising God and enjoying the favor of all the people. And the Lord added to their number daily those who were being saved. (Acts 2:42–47)

The word *fellowship* in verse 42 is translated from the Greek word *koinonia*; in other words, the very first Christian church was a St. Patricksy kind of place! The heartbeat of the life and ministry of Pat—who, of course, was only doing his best to emulate the life and ministry of Jesus Christ—was that every man, woman, or child who feels like a misfit can *belong* in the family of God through faith in Jesus Christ. The "body of Christ" is not a religious metaphor; it is the fruit and fuel of our faith. It's what Jesus was willing to die for, which is underscored by Paul's use of *koinonia* when he was describing the sacrament of communion to those mistake-prone Christians in Corinth:

> Is not the cup of thanksgiving for which we give thanks a *participation* [koinonia] in the blood of Christ? And is not the bread that we break a *participation* [koinonia] in the body of Christ? (1 Cor. 10:16)

■ **WHY *KOINONIA* MATTERS:** Christianity is relational, not transactional—it's about first getting to enjoy an authentic, intimate relationship with the God who breathed our universe into existence and then enjoying some measure of that relational intimacy with other image bearers. Koinonia represents the fact that our trinitarian God—whom Augustine described as existing as a community unto Himself—designed faith to be lived out in the context of community. Doing life *together* is a divine gift as well as a powerful witness to the watching world (see John 13:34).

31

Millennium

■ **MILLENNIUM:** One thousand years; in the Christian context, it is often understood as the thousand-year time period when Jesus Christ will rule upon the earth (after His second coming) before the end of world history as we know it.[1]

The term *millennium* is often bandied about in conversations, sermons, books, and podcasts about eschatology, but as with most things regarding the end times, it's a somewhat murky term that is understood and applied very differently among Christ followers. Louis Berkhof, who was a renowned systematic theologian prior to his death in 1957 and remains influential among spiritual leaders today (especially in the Reformed tradition), went so far as to issue a warning about it: "The doctrine of the millennium has never yet been embodied in a single Confession, and therefore cannot be regarded as a dogma of the Church."[2] However, many other pastors and theologians defend its use in light of its prominence in the following passage:

> And I saw an angel coming down out of heaven, having the key to the Abyss and holding in his hand a great chain. *He seized the dragon, that ancient serpent,*

1. Richard H. Hiers, "Millennium," in *HarperCollins Bible Dictionary*, 3rd ed., ed. Mark Allan Powell (HarperCollins, 2011), 636.
2. Louis Berkhof, *The History of Christian Doctrines* (Baker, 1975), 264.

> *who is the devil, or Satan, and bound him for a thousand years.* He threw him into the Abyss, and locked and sealed it over him, to keep him from deceiving the nations anymore *until the thousand years were ended.* After that, he must be set free for a short time.
>
> I saw thrones on which were seated those who had been given authority to judge. And I saw the souls of those who had been beheaded because of their testimony about Jesus and because of the word of God. They had not worshiped the beast or its image and had not received its mark on their foreheads or their hands. They came to life and reigned with Christ *a thousand years.* (The rest of the dead did not come to life *until the thousand years were ended.*) This is the first resurrection. Blessed and holy are those who share in the first resurrection. The second death has no power over them, but they will be priests of God and of Christ and will reign with him *for a thousand years.*
>
> *When the thousand years are over,* Satan will be released from his prison and will go out to deceive the nations in the four corners of the earth—Gog and Magog—and to gather them for battle. In number they are like the sand on the seashore. They marched across the breadth of the earth and surrounded the camp of God's people, the city he loves. But fire came down from heaven and devoured them. And the devil, who deceived them, was thrown into the lake of burning sulfur, where the beast and the false prophet had been thrown. They will be tormented day and night for ever and ever. (Rev. 20:1–10)

This passage in Revelation makes the eschatological context of the term *millennium* clear, but it's also where the rubber meets the road of dissention because people of faith have vigorously disagreed in their interpretations of John's vision pretty much since he wrote it down. Modern theologian Michael F. Bird aptly truncates the dispute over *millennium* into two questions: (1) Should the thousand years be taken literally or metaphorically? (2) What does the millennium actually signify?[3]

3. Michael F. Bird, *Evangelical Theology: A Biblical and Systematic Introduction*, 2nd ed. (Zondervan, 2020), 333.

Which brings us to the three most common *macro* views regarding the *millennium* (among which there are many iterations, and these doctrinal waters are further muddied when the term *millennium* is interchanged with the term *tribulation* because they are not technically interchangeable):

- *Premillennialism*: This is the doctrinal view that Christ's second coming will occur *before* the millennium, at which time He will rule over the nations for a thousand years until history ends. Although not the only interpretation during the first three centuries of the Christian era, premillennialism was the earliest and most dominant position of the church. It declined during the Constantinian and medieval periods, but it attracted widespread attention once again during the nineteenth century and remains very popular today, especially among Christian fundamentalists and conservative evangelicals worldwide.
- *Postmillennialism*: This is the doctrinal view that Jesus will return *after* the millennial golden age, when good progressively triumphs over evil because of the spread of the gospel and of Christian influence on society. Scholars are in disagreement regarding its origins, but some of its basic ideas were anticipated early in Christian history.
- *Amillennialism*: This is the doctrinal view that rejects the very idea of a future earthly millennium—a literal thousand-year period in history—and instead interprets John's vision symbolically as Christ's reign from heaven in the present church age. Amillennialism waned in influence with the rise of millennial views in the eighteenth and nineteenth centuries, but since the latter half of the twentieth century, it has been gaining in theological popularity. Among Eastern Orthodox, Roman Catholic, and mainline Protestant denominations, it is probably the most widely held position.

Whether you're a premillennialist, a postmillennialist, an amillennialist, or simply befuddled by all these *millennial* terms because your only association with the end times comes from the Hunger Games movies, the millennial Maypole we can all rally around is that while Jesus commands His followers to *keep watch* for His return (He uses the imperatives to "be on guard," "be alert," or "keep watch" seven times in Mark 13 during a conversation with His disciples about the end times), we don't have to *worry*. Because the King of all kings *is* coming back for us. And when He does, there will be no more cancer. No more child abuse. No more human trafficking. No more ethnic "cleansing." No more racial profiling. No more political discord. No more divorce. No more pornography. No more ghosting. No more gossiping. No more dying. No more crying. We don't have to live as fearful victims because, through His sacrificial death and subsequent resurrection, Jesus has *already* ensured the victory!

- **WHY *MILLENNIUM* MATTERS:** Although there's only one explicit biblical reference to the millennium (Rev. 20:1–15), the concept of Jesus returning to establish a thousand-year reign continues to permeate eschatological doctrine and thinking. Quite frankly, it would be very difficult to have a deep conversation about the end times without using or hearing the term *millennium*. Therefore, whether your eschatological viewpoint includes a literal thousand-year reign, a figurative thousand-year reign, or you believe John's vision was purely prophetic symbolism, it still behooves you to know the meaning of this term in order to have *meaningful conversations about God* (the very essence of theology!)—including the return of Jesus Christ and our ultimate inheritance of heaven (or hell for unbelievers)—with other image bearers.

32

Orthodoxy

■ **ORTHODOXY:** *Ortho* is a Greek prefix that means "right" or "correct," and *dox* means "belief"—therefore, in the Christian context, the word *orthodoxy* refers to the "right beliefs" about God.

Most Christians have two theologies. We have a *formal theology*, which could be loosely described as the statement of faith that hangs in our church's foyer or is written on their website. If your church includes liturgy in worship, it might also be expressed in a corporate confession like the Apostles' Creed. It's how we would answer the question—provided it's posed by someone who truly wants to know—"What are your personal beliefs about God and spirituality?" *Formal theology* is basically a layman's term for *orthodoxy* (right beliefs about God).

Whereas our *functional theology* is how we live our everyday lives when we're *not* worshiping in church, engaging in a Christ-centered small group, or attending a Christian concert or faith-based event. It's basically a layman's term for *orthopraxy* and *orthopathy* (how we live, act, and feel in light of what we believe to be true about God—don't worry, we're about to explore those concepts too!). Although our formal theology and our functional theology are not synonymous, they should overlap. Because the areas where they don't overlap become seedbeds of hypocrisy. *If what we believe to be true of God doesn't change the shape of our heart and how we live our life, then it's simply a conceptual idea.*[1] And unfortunately, when we mix mere conceptual ideas and religious fervor, people get really hurt and end up limping away from the proverbial pond of Christianity.

About fifteen years ago, I'd just finished teaching the Bible at a conference and was praying with some precious saints who'd come to the altar when I came face-to-face with an angry, Bible-waving woman. Her formal theology was likely "orthodox," based on the giant Bible she was swinging around, but her informal theology revealed itself to be severely lacking when it came to the last—and arguably the most important—command Jesus gave His disciples before His crucifixion and resurrection: "Love one another" (John 13:34).

She aggressively inserted herself between me and the women I'd been praying with and then unleashed a verbal tirade. She was so mad, spittle formed at the corners of her mouth and I couldn't quite understand what she was saying, apart from a few King James verse fragments and the word *Jezebel*, which she kept repeating over and over again. I thought she might be having some kind of seizure and motioned for one of the leaders so they could call 911 because my phone was still in my purse on a pew somewhere.

But then I realized she was calling *me* a Jezebel. It took several of us several minutes to decipher every word she spewed, but eventually it became clear that she was furious about what I'd worn to church. Because it was a cold winter day, I'd worn knee-high boots and a wool skirt that fell well below my knees. On top of my almost-Amish bottom half, I was wearing a loose-fitting, long-sleeved, pastel-colored sweater set. Honestly, I could've worn that same outfit to a convent and no one would've blinked an eye. Mind you, I knew beforehand that most of the audience were older gals from a very conservative denomination, and while I'm not the sharpest tool in the shed, I'm neither a masochist nor a complete idiot. Thank goodness I hadn't ridden my motorcycle

---

1. Jim Howard and Donald Payne, syllabus and teaching notes, Biblical and Theological Reflection on the Practice of Ministry, Denver Seminary, July 2019.

because then I would've worn leather pants, and that woman surely would've tried to have me stoned!

I think Francis Schaeffer framed orthodoxy best when he said, "There is nothing more ugly than a Christian orthodoxy without understanding or without compassion."[2] It behooves us all to remember that the Bible isn't a rule book; it's a divine love story. Therefore, correct beliefs about God should always fall under the canopy of His compassion. And within the context of a compassionate relationship with our Creator Redeemer, the boundaries He graciously put in place for us aren't punitive; they're promissory.

> LORD, you alone are my portion and my cup;
> you make my lot secure.
> The boundary lines have fallen for me in pleasant places;
> surely I have a delightful inheritance.
> I will praise the LORD, who counsels me;
> even at night my heart instructs me.
> I keep my eyes always on the LORD.
> With him at my right hand, I will not be shaken. (Ps. 16:5–8)

■ **WHY *ORTHODOXY* MATTERS:** Because it represents "right beliefs" about God—based on biblical truisms—that have established universal and unifying norms for Christ followers and Christian churches. Orthodoxy gives believers sound theological scaffolding on which we can build our belief system, as opposed to allowing Christianity to be shaped by our personal preferences and opinions.

2. Francis A. Schaeffer, *The God Who Is There* (InterVarsity, 1968), 54.

33

Orthopathy

■ **ORTHOPATHY:** *Ortho* is a Greek prefix that means "right" or "correct" (think of how we go to an *ortho*dontist to correct crooked teeth or an *ortho*pedist to correct musculoskeletal problems). And *pathos* generally means "feelings" or "emotion"—therefore, in the Christian context, the word *orthopathy* refers to the "right feelings" in light of what we believe to be true about God. This term was coined by Dr. Richard Mouw, who was the president of Fuller Theological Seminary from 1993 to 2013.

Again, it's imperative for us to consider this theological concept in triplicate context—as one of the three legs needed to balance the stool of Christoformity (living a life that's shaped like Jesus). Because *orthopathy* expressed apart from its symbiotic siblings, *orthodoxy* (right beliefs about God) and *orthopraxy* (right actions in light of what we believe to be true about God), is about as useful as a sectional in a tiny house!

Speaking of houses feeling tiny, we got a new dog (our third) a couple of summers ago because these sweet kids were selling happy, healthy-looking, blond, and boisterous puppies (their homemade sign advertised them as goldendoodles) at the edge of a Buc-ee's parking lot, and I just couldn't resist, especially after Missy held him and declared, "Mom, I already love him, and he already loves me!" I called our vet on the way home and confessed that I might have been suckered into a wolf with worms.

Bucky (what else could we name him?) has grown into a fluffy, super-sweet, fifty-two-pound 'doodle who only has two flaws: The first is his firmly held belief that he's a *micro*doodle. His self-identification as a tiny dog is constantly revealed through his habit of hurling his huge, furry self on top of Missy and me whenever he has the chance and then smothering us with sloppy kisses. The second is that he more than lives up to the nickname Missy gave him soon after we brought him home—Sir Poops-a-Lot.

Since he's technically Missy's dog, we agreed that the heavy lifting of house-training him should fall on her teenage shoulders. She was, of course, very enthusiastic about that arrangement in the Buc-ee's parking lot while begging me to buy him. However, once she had to start getting up with him at six o'clock every morning, her enthusiasm waned. So much so that one time she flat-out refused to get up for his morning ritual. Which led to an unwanted deposit on a brand-new rug, which led to an animated mother-and-daughter "discussion." Which led to my normally very sweet, very kind, and very respectful kid pitching a fit and mumbling, "Sometimes I wish you weren't my mom."

"Sometimes I wish you weren't my mom." Dang, I went through heck and back for years, spent everything I had financially and emotionally, to adopt her from Haiti after her first mama died. I have given my daughter most of the real estate of my heart. Frankly, I don't think it even resides in my chest anymore. The moment I stepped off an old diesel-spewing bus on a dirt road in a primitive Haitian village in the spring of 2012 and her great-aunt Fifi placed her in my arms, I was completely smitten. Still am.

She's my first priority after Jesus every single minute of every single day, and yet she has the audacity to whine about trading me in for a newer, more lenient parent just because of a little poo? Gee whiz, I hadn't even had my coffee before she hurled that harpoon into the softest part of my soul! Of course, it stung a smidge, but she is, after all, a sleep-deprived teenager, which means hordes of uninvited gangs of hormones are racing up and down the streets of her precious self all hours of the day and night. I knew she didn't really mean what she said. Which was exactly what she whispered through tears during a long hug a few minutes after the meltdown.

I've made so many parenting mistakes since becoming her second mama twelve and a half years ago, but the one thing I've done relatively well is give my daughter room to grow up. To stretch into everything God has gifted and called her to be. I know I'm pathologically biased, but Missy really is a very kind and very respectful young woman. Given the scarcity and trauma of her early years, it would make sense if she was a disingenuous people pleaser like most abuse survivors who typically struggle with serious abandonment issues. Like I was when I was her age. Instead, by the pure grace of God, Missy is gut-level honest. She doesn't curate her emotions with me because she's learned she doesn't need to present the shiniest version of herself for me to keep her. Her position as my kid is more secure than two pairs of Spanx. She will never not be my daughter, and I will always love her.

That's the key to orthopathy—to expressing the right *feelings* in light of our faith in God. We don't have to curate our emotions, y'all, because our position as His beloved children is *secure*. We can share *everything* with Him—our joy, our tears, our hopes, our dreams, our insecurities, our anger, our fears—we even get to have moments when we shake our tiny, all-too-human fists and complain about His parenting, all in the absolute confidence that He will never leave us or forsake us or stop loving us. Let's remove "Fake it 'til you make it" from our repertoire. Let's resolve to never again slap on a happy face when our hearts are broken. The *right* emotions for us to express—in light of what we believe to be true about our Creator Redeemer—are the *real* ones.

> Cast all your anxiety on him because he cares for you. (1 Pet. 5:7)

- **WHY *ORTHOPATHY* MATTERS:** Because human beings are not just brains with legs—God created us to be emotional beings as well! Orthopathy recognizes that feelings aren't "unspiritual" or extraneous but can be a viable means through which we live out our faith in the context of relationship with God and other image bearers.

34

Orthopraxy

■ **ORTHOPRAXY:** *Ortho* is a Greek prefix that means "right" or "correct," and *praxis* generally means "activity"—therefore, in the Christian context, the word *orthopraxy* refers to the "right actions" in light of what we believe to be true about God.

It's best to consider this oh-so-important spiritual concept as one of a set of triplets, with the symbiotic siblings being *orthodoxy* (right beliefs about God) and *orthopathy* (right feelings in light of what we believe to be true about God). In order to be imitators of Christ (see 1 Cor. 11:1; Eph. 5:1), to be His ambassadors to a lost and broken world (see 2 Cor. 5:20), and to live the abundant life Jesus's incarnation, crucifixion, and resurrection give us miraculous access to (see John 10:10), these three theological concepts must operate in unison with each other like a harmonious three-piece band. Otherwise, the effect won't just be discordant, orthopraxy will shape-shift into a pied piper with a heretical flute whose tune lures us in the opposite direction of where our unconditionally loving God leads.

But let me warn you from personal experience, the horn of orthopraxy is easy to toot all by yourself. Especially if you're a grade-A, certified people pleaser like I was for much of my life. Because my dad left us for another woman when I was four years old, and some men posing as "uncles" sexually molested me in the sad, chaotic wake that crashed over our little fractured family after my parents' divorce, I believed the lie that I was dirty and damaged for decades. I put my faith in Jesus when I was five and therefore knew at a very elementary level that He'd "saved" me from my sins. But I secretly thought He *had to* in order to fulfill His job description as the Messiah.

Therefore, since I was convinced that God had to lower the bar to let me into His kingdom, I resolved to do my very best to be a "good girl" so that He wouldn't regret the decision to deliver me. From my earliest memories, *worth* and *work* were congruent—I woke up every morning thinking, "I've got to *do better* today," and the mantra that played constantly in my head was, "I don't deserve this; I need to try harder." I grew into a dutiful Christ follower, comfortable *doing* things for God, but the fact that He *delights* in me, even on my nonproductive days—well, that truth was elusive for a long time.

It's taken a Porsche's worth of Christian counseling and lots of overtime on Holy Spirit's part for me to finally untangle my worth from my work. Along the way, I've learned that many of us in the family of faith struggle with performative behavior because the world usually applauds the most productive people the loudest. We're the ones who make the all-state teams and honor rolls and crush the sales quota. We're the ones pastors recognize as "necessary volunteers" if our churches are going to flourish. So it's natural for us to get our work and our worth tangled up. It makes sense that we're prone to prioritize the "go out and do" passages more than the "be still and know" parts. It's almost as if we've been conditioned to believe all our activity "on God's behalf" is adding up like some kind of divine frequent flyer miles. That our spiritual practices will somehow offset our sinful culpability.

Which is why it's helpful to hyper-focus on the last two syllables of *orthopraxy*. Because *praxis* is as different from *practice* as a canned biscuit is from a scratch-made one! Because unlike *practice,* which can describe rote behavior, like practicing one's multiplication tables or parallel parking skills, *praxis* refers to an action in which there is inherent meaning that reflects the motive of one's heart. For example, giving a gift for the sole reason of getting something back in return isn't actually giving a "gift" because, by definition, a gift is free.[1] The bottom line is, *praxis* means our hearts are engaged in the activity too. We're not working because we're trying to earn something from God or appease Him; our actions are in direct response to the amazing grace He's already lavished on us. Our "good deeds" are really just a massive "Thanks, Dad!" So, we can happily hum and genuinely grin while we're doing *whatever* it is we're doing because the Creator of the Universe is the one clapping for us, waving at us, and holding a huge sign that says "That's MY kid!" True orthopraxy is a "want to," not a "have to."

- **WHY *ORTHOPRAXY* MATTERS:** Because it is how we live our faith out loud—orthopraxy connects the dots between theological understanding and lived experience. Jesus's brother James explains it well:

> What good is it, my brothers and sisters, if someone claims to have faith but has no deeds? Can such faith save them? Suppose a brother or a sister is without clothes and daily food. If one of you says to them, "Go in peace; keep warm and well fed," but does nothing about their physical needs, what good is it? In the same way, faith by itself, if it is not accompanied by action, is dead. (James 2:14–17)

In other words, faith in God should prompt us to radical, Jesus-shaped actions.

1. Dr. Don Payne, syllabus and teaching notes, Biblical and Theological Reflection on the Practice of Ministry, Denver Seminary, July 2019.

35

Parousia

■ **PAROUSIA:** *Parousia* literally means "presence after absence" or "arrival" and typically refers to Jesus Christ's second advent or second coming.[1]

The exact phraseology "second advent" or "second coming" isn't used in the New Testament to describe Jesus Christ's return to earth (it wasn't until the second century that ancient theologian Justin Martyr differentiated Jesus's first coming from His second coming[2]), but the fact that *He is coming back* is prophesied numerous times—many of which are associated with Him judging the world at the end of this age (see 1 Cor. 1:8; 5:5; 15:23; 2 Cor. 1:14; Phil. 1:6, 10; 2:16; 1 Thess. 2:19; 3:13; 4:15; 5:2, 23; 2 Thess. 2:1–2; James 5:7; 2 Pet. 1:16; 3:4, 12; 1 John 2:28). But for those of us who've put our hope and faith in Jesus Christ as Lord and Savior, His *Parousia* is something to look forward to, not to fear. It underscores the theological truisms that He already came once in incarnate form to offer redemption for humanity, and He's coming back a second time to claim those who've been redeemed.

1. Bird, *Evangelical Theology*, 2nd ed., 319.
2. Michael F. Bird, *Evangelical Theology: A Biblical and Systematic Introduction* (Zondervan, 2013), 259–60.

Missy had only been home from Haiti for two weeks when I took her to her first Christian women's conference. (I'd scheduled a three-month sabbatical to give her time to adjust to life in America with me, but because of things outside of my control in her home country, Missy's arrival date kept getting pushed back.) I can still remember how tiny she was at that event—although she was four and a half years old, she'd been so sick and malnourished that she looked more like a two-year-old. But she was a *strong* little peanut, because whenever we were around a lot of people and she got anxious, she'd wrap her teeny arms around my neck and her legs around my waist like a barnacle, and it was all but impossible to peel her off—not that I wanted to!

Anyway, that particular women's conference took place in an arena with around ten thousand women in attendance, so it's safe to say Missy wasn't the only one who was feeling overwhelmed! When the producer walked over to where we were standing backstage and explained they were about to introduce me and I needed to get ready to walk onstage, he gestured to Missy and asked, "Can someone else hold her?" My aunt Darlene (who'd just spent a few days in Tennessee with us getting to know Missy) was standing right there with a gentle smile and outstretched arms, but when I asked Missy in broken Creole if she was okay for me to let her go for a little while, she shook her head back and forth solemnly and whispered, "Missy go with manman blan [which means 'white mama' in Creole]." So I smiled down at her, gave her a squeeze, and whispered back, "Okay, baby." Then I hitched her up a little higher to ensure she wouldn't slide off—along with my skirt!—and walked onstage to preach with my miracle of a daughter attached to my hip.

It took Missy a while to feel safe if I wasn't holding her when we were around other people. And it took her a bit longer to feel safe if I wasn't in the same room where she was. But pretty soon she learned that I would *always* come back for her. Even on those rare occasions when I had to travel for work and leave her with a family member (or "framily" member—those folks you're so close to, they *should* be kin) for a day or two so she didn't miss school, she learned that the second my job was done I'd fly back to her like a caffeinated homing pigeon. Now that Missy's a teenager, I'm pleasantly surprised she doesn't ask me to travel without her more often. I'm so grateful she still enjoys going on the road with me. But I'm also grateful she's not afraid in my absence anymore. Because my girl knows in the marrow of her beautiful Haitian bones that her mama's return is imminent. Which is exactly the posture that *Parousia* should provoke in us—a confident, non-anxious expectancy that Jesus *will absolutely* come back for us.

- **WHY *PAROUSIA* MATTERS:** Because it helps us keep our eyes on the penultimate "prize" of the return of Jesus Christ. It reflects an eschatological awareness, which infuses our lives here on earth with evangelical purpose—that is, while the imminent Parousia of Jesus Christ is comforting for Christ followers, it means eternal damnation and separation from God for those who haven't yet put their hope in Him. Therefore, we must be alert and always ready to share the hope that lies within us (see 1 Pet. 3:15).

36

Perichoresis

■ **PERICHORESIS:** Comes from two Greek words—*peri*, which means "around," and *chorea*, which means "dance." *Perichoresis* is a theological term referring to the mutual indwelling and intersecting of the three persons of the Godhead and, if anything, helps in some ways to better clarify the concept of the Trinity. It is a term that expresses intimacy between the persons of the Godhead.[1]

From the very beginning of our relationship, Missy and I have danced together. Within an hour or so of meeting her in a rural Haitian village—just a few months after her first mom, Marie, died—I played her an upbeat song on my phone and began to gyrate wildly to the music in a no-holds-barred attempt to make her smile. She was understandably wary but couldn't help giggling while watching me wiggle as rivulets of perspiration ran down my face, dripped off my elbows, and soaked the back of my hair because it was well over 100 degrees and the humidity was about 95 percent. Frankly, I think anyone who had the misfortune of watching my first routine in Haiti would've laughed out loud because I resembled a herky-jerky human sprinkler! However, within moments, Missy

1. Stephen M. Smith, "Perichoresis," in *Evangelical Dictionary of Theology*, ed. Daniel J. Treier and Walter A. Elwell (Baker Academic, 2017), 654.

climbed down from her aunt Fifi's lap and joined my sweaty, extemporaneous stomp-twirl-swivel fest. And we've had boogie fever ever since.

We dance down the aisles in grocery stores, we dance up and down trails when we're hiking, we wobbly-dance on top of pool floats, we dance in her school parking lot, and we have a habit of turning up the music at home while wearing socks so we can slide-dance on the hardwood floors. Now that she's sixteen, sometimes my daughter is a tad less enthusiastic about dancing with me in public places like an airport concourse or a Buc-ee's. But even when she rolls her eyes over my antics, there's still a twinkle in them. Recently, after a belly-laugh-inducing dance in our hotel room during a trip to California, Missy proclaimed with a happy sigh, "Mom, even though you'll be really old when I get married and have kids of my own, we'll still dance together because it's *our thing*!" In other words, moving our bodies in tandem to music (she much more rhythmically than I) exemplifies our mother-daughter bond. We may not share the same DNA, but our symbiotic predilection to boogie proves our familial roots run deep!

While the biblical truism of the Trinity is one of the main walls of Christian orthodoxy, it's a very complex subject—as evidenced by how it was argued over for centuries by ancient Christian leaders throughout the ecumenical councils. Saint Augustine once observed, "There is no subject where error is more dangerous, research more laborious, and discovery more fruitful than the oneness of the Trinity [unitas trinitatis] of the Father, the Son, and the Holy Spirit."[2] And despite two thousand years of argument and rigorous study by theologians, academics, and seminary professors, the big-*C* Christian church still hasn't landed on a theological consensus. Nor has anyone found the perfect model or metaphor to describe the Trinity.

I used to think using H_2O was a decent example to explain the Trinity—it made sense to me as a kid in Sunday school, so I continued using it when I

2. Quoted in Bird, *Evangelical Theology*, 2nd ed., 108–9.

began working in youth ministry. It wasn't until my second go-round in seminary that I realized that the familiar H_2O illustration I'd used for decades is an unfortunate example of *modalism,* which is a flawed doctrinal view that there is one God who has sequentially revealed himself as Father, Son, and Holy Spirit, yet each divine name is merely a mode of the one God's activity as opposed to a distinct person.[3] Since water, ice, and steam all come from the exact same compound (H_2O), it may seem to be a symbolic slam dunk for God the Father, God the Son, and God the Spirit. However, since water can't simultaneously exist as ice, ice can't simultaneously exist as steam, and steam can't simultaneously exist as water, this whole watery model evaporates (pun intended) when you apply the heat of logic to it.

I fell hard for the term *perichoresis* the first time I heard one of my seminary professors explain it because it's the first illustration I've heard used to describe the Trinity that "held water" (sorry, couldn't resist). Ancient church father John of Damascus began using this Greek term in the eighth century. In his brilliant work *De fide orthodoxa,* he explained that the three persons of the Trinity "are made one not so as to commingle, but so as to cleave to each other, and they have their being in each other without any coalescence or commingling."[4] Since our English word *choreography* is derived from the Greek root word *choresis,* some pastors and teachers now use dance as a metaphor to describe the Trinity. Perichoresis is probably better understood as a circle of perpetual movement, but the image of God the Father, God the Son, and God the Spirit joyfully boogying down some grocery store aisle together in Glory is compelling, isn't it?

Modern scholar Kevin DeYoung explains the profound concept of perichoresis much better (and more appropriately) than I can:

> The Greek term used to describe the eternal mutual indwelling of the persons of the Trinity is *perichoresis* (in Latin, *circumincession*). The word *circulatio* is

3. Bird, *Evangelical Theology,* 2nd ed., 110.
4. John of Damascus, *De fide orthodoxa* 1.8, PG 94.829A.

> also sometimes used as a way of metaphorically describing the unceasing circulation of the divine essence, such that each person is in the other two, while the others are in each one. At the risk of putting things in physical terms, perichoresis means that "all three persons occupy the same divine space." In other words, we cannot see God without seeing all three persons at the same time.[5]

"We cannot see God without seeing all three persons at the same time." Our Creator Redeemer is a supernatural, synergistic blur of unparalleled power and unconditional love. And we are divinely designed to fit smack-dab in the middle of that blur!

- **WHY *PERICHORESIS* MATTERS:** Because the more we can wrap our finite minds around the infinite miracle of the Trinity, the more we'll be able to enjoy the rhythm of communion with God (our heavenly Father), Jesus the Son (our Savior), and the Holy Spirit (our Comforter). Our hearts will wear out quickly from solo dancing, but when we place our tiny human feet on top of His Divine-Daddy oxfords and lift our arms up to be held, we're swept into a wonderful sort of waltz that lasts forever.

5. Kevin DeYoung, "Theological Primer: Perichoresis," The Gospel Coalition, November 19, 2020, https://www.thegospelcoalition.org/blogs/kevin-deyoung/theological-primer-perichoresis/.

37

Pharisee

■ **PHARISEE:** This word comes from the Greek word *pharisaios,* which means "separate ones." The Pharisees emerged as a recognizable group in Jewish culture during the second century BC and remained prominent throughout the New Testament era, distinguished by their notable leaders and distinctive lifestyle. Membership was not inherited but achieved by pledging to lead a pure life according to the group's strict rules. They held regular meetings led by scribes, who were considered the best Scripture scholars, and took leadership roles as rabbis and authorized teachers in synagogues.[1]

The majority of Jewish people during the time period of Jesus's earthly ministry were just regular blue-collar folks trying to eke out a living as farmers or shepherds. The Hebrew term for those everyday people is *'am ha'aretz,* which literally means "people of the land." Most men, women, and children among the 'am ha'aretz didn't have the luxury of a formal education and were illiterate. Therefore, since they couldn't read the Torah for themselves, they had to trust the Pharisees, an educated sect of Jewish men who were influential during the

1. John A. Beck, *The Baker Illustrated Guide to Everyday Life in Bible Times* (Baker Books, 2013), 186.

Second Temple period (from the second century BC until the latter part of the first century AD), to interpret it for them.

Based on biblical narrative, some of the Pharisees (it's important to note that not all Pharisees were demeaning, divisive, or disingenuous; Nicodemus and Joseph of Arimathea were both Pharisees, and they are portrayed positively in the Gospels) were like overzealous school crossing guards with giant whistles when it came to being the liaisons between the Jewish people and Jehovah because they were persnickety about applying the Torah (the first of three divisions of the Hebrew Scriptures, which is now part of our Old Testament canon) to every single facet of life. They spent inordinate amounts of time hunched over copies of the Mosaic law in order to codify six-hundred-plus biblical imperatives. Then they used their strict interpretations of God's Law to impose rigid behavioral standards among the common people.

They had vigorous debates about what types of food you could or couldn't eat, how to cut your hair, how to bandage blisters, and when you could or couldn't be physically intimate with your spouse. They were obsessive about religious policy but obtuse about a personal relationship with God, which Jesus laments in John 5:39–40:

> You study the Scriptures diligently because you think that in them you have eternal life. These are the very Scriptures that testify about me, yet you refuse to come to me to have life.

These dudes posted selfies from their Christian cruises, but instead of demonstrating compassion toward others and intimacy with God, they epitomized spiritual pride. And in the following passage, Jesus rebukes them for showboating orthodoxy sans compassion. For being great pretenders who don't practice what they preach:

> Woe to you, teachers of the law and Pharisees, *you hypocrites*! You clean the outside of the cup and dish, but inside they are full of greed and

> self-indulgence. Blind Pharisee! First clean the inside of the cup and dish, and then the outside also will be clean.
>
> Woe to you, teachers of the law and Pharisees, *you hypocrites*! You are like whitewashed tombs, which look beautiful on the outside but on the inside are full of the bones of the dead and everything unclean. In the same way, on the outside you appear to people as righteous but on the inside you are full of hypocrisy and wickedness. (Matt. 23:25–28)

To say that Jesus stepped on their toes with this stinging public rebuke is an epic understatement. And the Pharisees weren't just embarrassed by this confrontation; it was the catalyst for them to start planning His murder. And the word He used that likely sparked their entitled religiosity into homicidal rage was *hypocrite*. *Hypocrite* is a Greek term found only in the Gospels of Matthew, Mark, and Luke, and our Savior is the only one who speaks it. No one else in the entirety of Holy Writ uses it. *Hypocrite* is a Greek word that means "actor," and Jesus used this theatrical expression to accuse the Pharisees of some serious spiritual make-believe!

There's probably no other word that would have been more offensive to the Pharisees' egotistical ears because they had nothing but disdain for actors. Theater was a pagan Greek phenomenon—a culture religious Jews viewed as immoral and abhorrent. Yet they were surrounded by it because by the time of Christ, the Greeks had conquered much of the ancient world (followed by the Romans, who adopted the Greek/Hellenistic way of life), so their licentious culture had become the norm in most civilized nations, including Israel.

The Greeks and Romans violated the holy laws of the Torah in every way, shape, and form. Instead of worshiping Jehovah, the one true God, they practiced polytheism, worshiping the numerous "gods" of the Greek pantheon, and threw a pinch of astronomy and astrology into their belief system for good measure. They were moral anarchists whose basic creed was "If it feels good, do it!" And the theater was the centerpiece of their lascivious lifestyle. Many ancient Greek plays featured full nudity, with actors engaging in all kinds of pornographic behavior.

Therefore, when Jesus called the religious leaders of His day hypocrites—*actors!*—I imagine the crowd gasped and the Pharisees within earshot sputtered while turning bright red. The Messiah insulted those religious poseurs in the worst possible way. No one had ever dared to speak to them like that before. So why did He?

The Son of God expressed righteous anger toward those Pharisees because their pretentious performance was making a mockery of the gospel. They insisted on following a formula instead of repenting and putting their faith in the forgiveness and mercy of God. Their dangerous game of pious make-believe led others to believe that they could never approach God, much less be loved by Him. I mean, good night, who could possibly check off every single item on a six-hundred-plus-item-long checklist of perfectly righteous behavior?

Their emphasis on legalism missed the point and pointed others in the wrong direction. Their acting skills were admirable, but their doctrine was defective. To keep their fig leaves of religious superiority in place, they established an impossible system of hierarchical hoops for others to jump through. They were much more concerned with *looking* spiritual than they were with loving God with all their hearts and loving their neighbors as themselves. Their formal theology and their functional theology were a million miles apart.

WHY *PHARISEE* MATTERS: Because using spirituality to gain a platform, prestige, power, or other people's approval is still a problem in modern-day culture. Those ancient spiritual leaders prove that religious zeal and a relationship with God are not synonymous. They effectively hold up a mirror for us to consider the motives of our own hearts, and studying the encounters Jesus had with oppositional Pharisees during His earthly ministry can help clarify how not to order the steps of our lives as His beloved!

38

Pneumatology

■ **PNEUMATOLOGY:** The theological term for the field of study pertaining to the Holy Spirit. The term is derived from the Greek root words *pneuma*, which means "spirit" or "breath," and *logos*, which means "word," "speech," "reason," or "principle."

What makes this theological term especially memorable is that both the Old Testament Hebrew word for "spirit"—*ruach*—and the New Testament Greek word for "spirit"—*pneuma*—are onomatopoeic terms. That means the sound made when saying the word conveys its basic definition—in this case, *the expulsion of wind* or *air in motion*. It's what a cartoonist does by doodling the word "Muah!" above a smooching couple to convey the sound of their kiss. How cool is it that the divinely inscripturated names given Holy Spirit express in the most fundamental way that He's the *breath* of life?

In the Old Testament, Holy Spirit is often referred to as "the Spirit of God," "the Spirit of the Lord," "the Spirit of the living God," and "My Spirit." However, the exact moniker—*Holy Spirit*—is mentioned several times in the Old Testament, too, such as when David begs Holy Spirit not to leave him after he gets busted having intimate relations with Bathsheba while she is still married to

Uriah the Hittite in Psalm 51, and again when the prophet Isaiah laments the consequences of Israel's rebellion in Isaiah 63.

Holy Spirit gets even more press in the New Testament. (After the sacrificial death and subsequent resurrection of Jesus, the rest of the Bible kind of becomes His highlight reel!) Numerous references laud how He enables us to confess the true identity of Christ and worship Him (1 Cor. 12:3; Eph. 2:18; Phil. 3:3), how He gives believers insight into divine mysteries (1 Cor. 2:10), and how He sanctifies and transforms us into a more Jesus-shaped image (1 Cor. 3:16; 2 Cor. 3:18). In light of all these incredible things Holy Spirit does for us, it's fitting He's been assigned a bevy of beautiful names in the New Testament, including Helper, Counselor, Comforter, and Advocate—all of which are translated from the Greek word *paraklētos,* which literally means "called to one's side."

However, it's also important to note that the field of pneumatology is full of wildly differing viewpoints regarding the Holy Spirit among theologians, and recent polls reveal Christ followers have more confusion and unbelief about the third member of the Trinity than they do about God the Father and God the Son.[1] Scottish theologian Dr. Sinclair Ferguson aptly explains our proclivity to be perplexed: "For while his work has been recognized, the Spirit himself remains to many Christians an anonymous, faceless aspect of the divine being. Even the title 'Holy Spirit' evokes a different gamut of emotions from those expressed in response to the titles of 'Father' and 'Son.'"[2]

Then there's another colorful reason to wrinkle our brows in confusion—worse still, belittle people whose pneumatology differs from our own—because one of the most well-known yet hotly debated gifts attributed to the Holy Spirit is speaking in tongues (from the Greek word *glossolalia—glóssa* means "tongue" and *lalia* means "talking"), which we read about in Acts 2:1–12.

1. Joe Carter, "Study: Majority of Self-Identified Christians Don't Believe the Holy Spirit Is Real," *The Gospel Coalition,* September 18, 2021, https://www.thegospelcoalition.org/article/christians-dont-believe-spirit/.

2. Sinclair Ferguson, *The Holy Spirit,* Contours of Christian Theology (InterVarsity Press, 1996), 16.

Immediately following the disciples' Spirit-imbued ability to speak in other tongues, Luke clarifies that the huge crowd of Jews who'd gathered in Jerusalem to celebrate Pentecost were from at least fifteen different nations. Therefore, they spoke at least fifteen different dialects or languages. And yet they understood *exactly* what the disciples were saying. The ethnic barriers that likely existed at the beginning of this international gathering quickly dissipated when the disciples were filled with the power of Holy Spirit and spoke in tongues because it was also a miraculous moment of *xenoglossia* (*xenos* is the Greek word for "foreigner," and *glóssa* is the Greek word for "tongue" or "language"), which means the words that sounded strange to the disciples as they were vocalizing them were heard and comprehended by that crowd of foreigners in their native language! So it was more of a hearing miracle than a speaking miracle, and as a result, thousands put their hope in the recently resurrected Jesus, and His two declarative promises from Acts 1 were fulfilled with jaw-dropping immediacy:

> *But you will receive power when the Holy Spirit has come upon you, and you will be my witnesses in Jerusalem* and in all Judea and Samaria, and to the end of the earth. (Acts 1:8 ESV)

Unfortunately, that phenomenal event in biblical history has also led to much discord and consternation among Christians because some brilliant theologians, wonderful pastors, Christian leaders, and committed Christ followers believe the only proper manifestation of tongues was when it occurred as *xenolalia*—a known language—as it occurred at the biblical event of Pentecost in the book of Acts. Therefore, they reason that it is no longer a valid sign or gift of Holy Spirit. The theological term for that doctrinal viewpoint is *cessationist*, because it asserts that supernatural tongues have ceased. There are scads of other brilliant theologians, wonderful pastors, Christian leaders, and committed Christ followers who believe that speaking in tongues is a relevant spiritual gift and think xenolalia occurred again after the phenomenon in Acts and still occurs in modern culture. Still other brilliant theologians, wonderful pastors, Christian leaders, and committed Christ followers are passionate that *glossolalia*—aka ecstatic speech that is not heard or comprehended as a known language—is a valid outward manifestation of the inward presence of Holy Spirit and is helpful for their private devotional experience, spiritual growth, and evangelistic zeal. And those are just a *few* of the *many* dissenting views of that *one* gift from Holy Spirit that exist under the umbrella of pneumatology.

The very real and present danger regarding the dramatically different Christian opinions on speaking in tongues—which is also referred to as "the baptism of the Holy Spirit"—isn't just that it can cause division, confusion, and elitism in the body of Christ, it's that it tends to make us forget about *all the other gifts* that are ours through God's indwelling Spirit. Transformative stuff like the love, joy, peace, patience, kindness, goodness, faithfulness, gentleness, and self-control that are tangible "fruits" of the Holy Spirit, according to Galatians 5. Plus, other passages describe the Holy Spirit as empowering, purifying, teaching, comforting, convicting, guiding, and reminding Christ followers that we have the right to call the Creator of the universe "Dad" (see Rom. 8:15).

Regardless of what your current opinion is about speaking in tongues, make sure it doesn't suck Holy Spirit's life-giving *wind* out of your sails and prevent you from enjoying *all* the blessings He offers.

■ **WHY *PNEUMATOLOGY* MATTERS:** Because it is necessary to better understand the trinitarian nature of God, Christian theology, and how we can be Christoformic lights in this dark world. Furthermore, since Jesus promised He would send the Holy Spirit to be our *Paraclete* (the one who comes alongside) after His ascension—"And I will ask the Father, and he will give you another advocate to help you and be with you forever—the Spirit of truth" (John 14:16–17)—pneumatology is crucial when it comes to accessing the empowered, abundant life Jesus died to provide for us.

39

Sabbath

■ **SABBATH:** Comes from the Hebrew word *shabbat,* which means "to cease" or "desist," which is why it refers to the weekly day of rest and abstention from work enjoined upon the Israelites. The origin for the Sabbath comes from Genesis 2:1–3, which speaks of God ceasing from the work of creation on the seventh day, blessing the day, and declaring it *holy.*[1] In orthodox Judaism, Shabbat/Sabbath serves as a sign of the covenant between God and Israel and is observed from sundown on Friday evening—with a special prayer and meal—until sundown on Saturday evening. Over time, as the early Christian community emerged, strict Sabbath observance diminished, and Sunday became the primary day of worship for Christians.

The word *sabbath* occurs over one hundred times in the Old Testament, mostly in the Pentateuch—the first five books of the Bible. It's used considerably less in the New Testament and is reframed by Jesus multiple times, who emphasized that Sabbath "was made for man" not vice versa (Mark 2:24–28). The first time it appears is in Exodus:

1. *HarperCollins Bible Dictionary,* rev. and updated ed. (2011), under "sabbath."

> Remember the Sabbath day by keeping it holy. Six days you shall labor and do all your work, but the seventh day is a sabbath to the LORD your God. On it you shall not do any work, neither you, nor your son or daughter, nor your male or female servant, nor your animals, nor any foreigner residing in your towns. For in six days the LORD made the heavens and the earth, the sea, and all that is in them, but he rested on the seventh day. Therefore *the LORD* blessed the Sabbath day and made it holy. (Exod. 20:8–11)

I used to tense up when I heard those verses read or paraphrased because when I was growing up, our mom was emphatic about keeping the Sabbath holy. Which for a Southern-Baptist-to-the-bone mama meant my sister Theresa and I had to use our inside voices while clad in a prissy dress and uncomfortable shoes for the better part of the day we spent at church (back when even kids had to sit on hard wooden pews). It also meant we couldn't swim in a two-piece bathing suit when we got home.

Thankfully, our backyard was surrounded by a privacy fence, so at least she allowed us to swim on hot Sunday afternoons, but we had to wear modest one-piece bathing suits because my sweet mama considered uncovered midsections—even in private—wholly inappropriate on *the Sabbath* (she always slowed down and lowered her voice when she emphatically spoke those two words, which made them sound all the more ominous to me when I was little).

Based on my dear, very well-intentioned mother's understanding of what Christians *couldn't* do on Sunday—no baring of belly buttons, no loud talking, no loud music, no lawn mowing, no playing freeze tag, no bike riding, no TV watching, no loitering at Burger King with friends—by the time I could read, I'd deduced that God was a serious disciplinarian, determined to make His children sober, non-cavorting rule followers.

It wasn't until my first go-around in seminary that I learned to read God's Old Testament "parameters" in the sociohistorical context in which they were given. And in that context, the Sabbath shifts from a seemingly punitive decree to a thoughtful gift given by a doting Father. Because remember, the Israelites were the original audience Exodus was written to, and they heard this "Sabbath sermon" immediately after following Moses out of Egypt after *four hundred years in captivity*. They were as wobbly as newborn calves when it came to this whole liberation thing because they had no experience or understanding of what freedom felt like. For as long as their grandparents and great-grandparents and great-great-grandparents could remember, they'd existed as slaves under the mostly cruel ownership of their arch enemies, the Egyptians. A Jewish slave's sole purpose in Egyptian captivity was to do the brutal, backbreaking work their overseers didn't want to do—like mixing mud and straw to make bricks and hauling heavy stones in the oppressive Middle Eastern heat. And there was no such thing as vacation days, sick leave, or working remotely back then either. A slave's workday began early and ended late *every single day*.

Imagine working until your hands are covered in thick calluses and your back is covered in fresh wounds and old scars from beatings. Most of your joints are misshapen from torturous labor from the time you were eight or nine years old until the day you die. There was no clear light at the end of the tunnel for an Israelite slave. Their only practical, immediate hope was for a master who wasn't sadistic.

Imagine being trapped for so long that you completely forget what freedom feels like. I can only imagine how shell-shocked those Hebrews were by the time they set up camp at the base of Mount Sinai shortly after watching the Egyptian army who was in hot pursuit of them get swallowed up by the Red Sea. Their entire lives had been spent as captives, and now suddenly their chains were gone, manna was raining down like donuts from heaven, and Yahweh was hovering over them like a protective parent.

Now meditate on these words again in The Living Bible translation (when I'm studying a particular passage, it helps to read it in multiple translations, and I also like to read it out loud):

> Remember to observe the Sabbath as a holy day. Six days a week are for your daily duties and your regular work, but the seventh day is a day of Sabbath rest before the Lord your God. On that day you are to do no work of any kind, nor shall your son, daughter, or slaves—whether men or women—or your cattle or your house guests. For in six days the Lord made the heaven, earth, and sea, and everything in them, and rested the seventh day; so he blessed the Sabbath day and set it aside for rest. (Exod. 20:8–11 TLB)

In other words: *You matter so much to Me that I don't want you to work your fingers to the bone anymore! Your work and your worth are no longer synonymous. So I've established a twenty-four-hour no-labor time period in which you can relax and be refueled by leaning fully into My presence. I want you to sleep late, linger in conversation with Me, enjoy great food with your family, share a few long-winded stories, and laugh at your children's jokes. You aren't slaves anymore; you're My beloved children, and every single moment of your life exists under the canopy of My grace—but you need to take regular breaks to remember it.*

I tend to be a burn-the-candle-at-both-ends kind of person, so I deeply appreciate the context of Sabbath as a tangible expression of God's care and concern for us. I'm also grateful that He didn't just mandate rest, He modeled it:

> By the seventh day God had finished the work he had been doing; so on the seventh day *he rested* from all his work. Then God blessed the seventh day and made it holy, because on it *he rested* from all the work of creating that he had done. (Gen. 2:2–3)

Isn't it comforting to know that our heavenly Father crashed out on a celestial couch after creating the universe? God makes it abundantly clear that busyness isn't a spiritual fruit. We aren't supposed to resemble manic hamsters on spinning wheels; we're supposed to resemble Him. Plus, Genesis 2 takes place before the Fall, so rest isn't an accommodation for human weakness; it's part of God's *perfect* plan for us! The Sabbath isn't a punitive decree from a megalomaniac trying to take all the fun out of mowing the lawn or swimming on Sunday . . . it's a divine *gift* for our *good*.

- **WHY *SABBATH* MATTERS:** Jesus advocated balance for believers, and like God the Father, He modeled it (see Mark 1:35 and Luke 4:42). Finding a happy medium between *going out and doing* and *being still and knowing* is critical for Christ followers if we're going to finish the race He's called us to run (see Heb. 12:1–2). Resting—learning to weave practical sabbaths into our schedules—isn't a punitive "rule"; it's God's generous endowment for our protection and perseverance.

40

The Septuagint

THE SEPTUAGINT: The translation of the Old Testament from Hebrew into Greek, read in the early church and often quoted by New Testament writers.

The Septuagint is the oldest surviving Greek translation of the Hebrew Scriptures (which include twenty-four books, some Aramaic language, and are also referred to as the Masoretic Text). The word *Septuagint* comes from the Latin word *septuaginta*, which means "seventy." The reason this particular imperfect translation of the original Hebrew Scriptures got that name is because legend held that those sacred texts (specifically the first five books of the Old Testament—the *Pentateuch*) were translated and collated by seventy-two Jewish scholars (six from each of the original twelve tribes).[1] Hence the title "seventy," as well as the reason the Septuagint is also referred to as LXX (Latin numerals that add up to seventy). Historians and scholars disproved the premise about seventy-two Jewish authors a long, long time ago, but the name Septuagint stuck.

One of the main reasons it's a good idea for modern Christ followers to be familiar with the existence of the Septuagint is that it's quoted throughout the

1. Melvin K. H. Peters, "Septuagint," in *The Anchor Yale Bible Dictionary*, vol. 5, *O–Sh*, ed. David Noel Freedman (Doubleday, 1992), 1093.

New Testament. Here's why: The entire sociohistorical context of the New Testament takes place under the rule of the Roman Empire. And Greek was the common language of the Roman Empire (just as English is in the United Kingdom or the United States), regardless of an ancient citizen's ethnic identity (Jew or Gentile). Furthermore, most of the early Christians (including Jewish converts to Christianity) didn't know how to speak or read Hebrew, so they couldn't understand the Old Testament in its original linguistic format. Therefore, when Paul and other early Christian leaders wanted to refer to a passage from the Hebrew Scriptures in a sermon or a letter, they had to use a Greek translation in order for their audience/readers to understand it.

Which leads us to a few more interesting facts for Bible nerds as we circle the Septuagint drain:

- The Septuagint/LXX was *the* Bible of the early Christian church. It was not secondary to any other scripture; it *was* Scripture! When Paul urged his audience to consider that all Scripture given by divine inspiration is profitable for doctrine, it was to the LXX, not the Hebrew, that attention was being called. And all those fancy theological words we enjoy tossing around in small groups, like *righteousness* and *propitiation,* come directly from the Septuagint![2]
- The Septuagint/LXX explains the way the Hebrew Bible was understood and interpreted in antiquity. To the degree that every translation is a commentary, the first translation of the Hebrew Bible provides insight into the art of translation of a sacred text and the subtle (and at times blatant) way in which it was reinterpreted in the process.[3]
- The Septuagint/LXX is cited often in the Gospels, especially Luke. *Remember, New Testament writers like Luke, Paul, Peter, James, and John*

2. S. K. Soderlund, "Septuagint," in *The International Standard Bible Encyclopedia,* vol. 4, *Q–Z,* revised, ed. Geoffrey W. Bromiley (Eerdmans, 1988), 400.
3. Peters, "Septuagint," in *Anchor Yale Bible Dictionary,* 1102.

didn't have the New Testament portion of Scripture that we now hold so dear because they were the ones God used to write it!

However, while the Septuagint is an incredibly important work that informed much of the New Testament as we know it, it's not a perfect translation of the original Hebrew Scriptures. (Don't worry, the Old Testament most of our English Bible translations are based on comes directly from the *original* Hebrew and Aramaic, so you can stop clenching.) It includes some books that aren't found in the Protestant Bible, as well as some additions to the original Hebrew passages. That means it's kind of like the wonderful *Message* Bible that the brilliant and eminently humble Eugene Peterson—who wrote *The Message* and whom I had the undeserved privilege of meeting before he passed away—referred to as a *paraphrase*, not a translation. Dr. Peterson explained that he wrote *The Message* so contemporary readers would have a more accessible and relatable version of the Bible. He tried to capture the essence and spirit of the original Scriptures, but he never intended it to be used as a *strict, literal* translation.[4] My guess is the authors of the Septuagint didn't either.

■ **WHY THE *SEPTUAGINT* MATTERS:** Besides the fact that it's quoted throughout the New Testament, it represents an extremely early text of the Old Testament, some of which dates all the way back to the third century BC! And that means the Septuagint gives us an ancient and authentic testimony to the biblical text. Furthermore, the Septuagint was the interpretation of the Hebrew Scriptures used by much of the early church for spreading God's Word in their predominantly Greek-speaking world, which means many of the beloved teachings and sermons from early Christianity were shaped and influenced by the unique nuances in the Septuagint.

4. Doug LeBlanc, "'I Didn't Want to Be Cute': Author Eugene Peterson Describes What Drove His Writing of *The Message*," *Christianity Today*, October 7, 2002, https://www.christianitytoday.com/2002/10/eugene-peterson-message; see also introduction to *The Message*.

41

The Seven Ecumenical Councils

THE SEVEN ECUMENICAL COUNCILS: The first seven ecumenical councils were significant gatherings of Christian bishops that addressed key theological issues and established important doctrines for the early church. These councils, held between AD 325 and 787, were considered universal in scope, and their decisions were widely accepted by most Christians.[1] The councils dealt with various theological controversies and heresies, aiming to establish consensus on Christian beliefs.[2]

I fell hard—literally and figuratively—for wakesurfing last summer. If you aren't familiar with this relatively new water sport, it originated in the 1950s and '60s when creative and/or bored surfers decided to try riding their boards behind boats but didn't really take off until the 1990s when boats were designed with internal ballast tanks/bags and underwater tabs dedicated to making large artificial waves. Other than a few bathing suit mishaps that were surely

1. Mark Nickens, *A Survey of the History of Global Christianity*, 2nd ed. (B&H Academic, 2020), 47.
2. Victor Vadney, *The Arrogant Journey: Hermeneutics and Church History* (Desert Willow Publishing, 2012), 139.

unpleasant for people close enough to see the parts of me that should never see the light of day, it's been the most enjoyable new hobby I've picked up in a long time. And I picked it up quickly—especially for a sixty-two-year-old chick! My friend Josh—a thirty-something dude who's a competitive wakesurfer—watched a video of me "surfing" recently and observed, "The reason you're so comfortable on a board is because you spent a lot of time waterskiing when you were younger, and your body intuitively knows the 'ground rules' of cruising behind a boat. You know how to respect the line between having an absolute blast and one of those epic falls when you ingest a gallon of lake water and maybe even bust a rib!" (Okay, so I did experience one exciting tumble that resulted in the teeniest of rib cracks, but I was able to sneeze pain-free again within just a few weeks.)

Much more important than the ground rules for safely engaging in water sports are the ground rules that have been established for us to engage with the God of the universe. And our need for "boundaried doctrine" when it comes to Christianity was clear from the get-go about two thousand years ago! Not long after the start of the Christian church, around AD 30, it became alarmingly apparent that our belief system desperately needed ground rules and guardrails to avoid gospel-distorting disasters. The first rogue theological waves were caused by misinformed preachers who were preaching heresy about Jesus being of a lesser nature than God. The resulting controversies and church divisions are noted often in New Testament narrative—especially in Paul's epistles. Which is why Emperor Constantine eventually demanded that all the Christian church bishops meet together in the city of Nicaea for the first formal ecumenical Christian council in AD 325 (*ecumenical* is a term derived from the Greek word *oikoumene*, meaning "the whole inhabited earth," and usually relates to unity among Christian churches[3]). The assignment he gave those ancient spiritual leaders was to prayerfully come up with parameters

3. Daniel L. Migliore, *Faith Seeking Understanding: An Introduction to Christian Theology*, 4th ed. (Eerdmans, 2023), 490.

of praxis for the Christian faith so it didn't go careening off a biblically sound course and experience an epic fall.

Constantine was the sixtieth emperor of Rome (he reigned from AD 306 to 337), but he was the *first* Christian emperor. He put his hope in Jesus Christ after having a dream/vision about Him the night before a huge military battle against his brother-in-law Maxentius (I encourage you to read the whole story if you haven't yet because it is super interesting). Anyway, while Constantine had plenty of flaws, it's hard to overstate the impact his conversion had on history because prior to his placing his allegiance in and putting his stamp of approval on Christianity, Christ followers made up a microscopic minority of the ancient world's population and were severely persecuted—often maimed and even martyred for their faith in the Roman Colosseum as a sadistic form of public "entertainment." In fact, many of the Roman emperors who preceded Constantine—wicked despots like Nero and Caligula—*ordered* the persecution of Christians. That means the beginning of our belief system—those three hundred years that followed the earthly ministry of Jesus Christ—was extremely difficult and dangerous for our ancestors of faith.

Modern theologian and seminary professor Dr. Bryan Litfin describes the shock and wonder that must've permeated the start of that first ecumenical council in Nicaea when Emperor Constantine—the most powerful man in the world at that time—asked the church bishops (some of whom had been horrifically tortured with hot irons and had their eyes gouged out because they refused to recant their faith in Jesus) for *their permission* before he took his seat: "Don't miss what Constantine was doing here. He was giving full imperial dignity to Christianity in the same way that pagan religion used to receive it, while at the same time humbling himself as a mere layman in the presence of clergy. Something very big was happening to the status of the Christian church in the public sphere. The bishops could only marvel at what they were seeing."[4]

4. Litfin, *Story of the Trinity*, 122.

Ultimately, something much bigger than a change in perception happened.

Those first seven ecumenical councils hammered out the guardrails and guidelines of our Christian faith with truisms like the Trinity and the hypostatic union. The scarred saints (sure, there were a few stinkers among them, but as a whole they were heroic) who limped to those formative gatherings over the course of four and a half centuries left behind a theological legacy that provides the deep roots through which our relationship with God is nurtured and stabilized. It is largely because of their rich history that we can now enjoy an abundant walk of faith without too many soul-bruising tumbles in the dangerous waters of relativism.

- **WHY *THE SEVEN ECUMENICAL COUNCILS* MATTER:** Because they were pivotal in defining and defending fundamental Christian doctrines. The wisdom of the councils—which was rooted in the revelation they received from God's Word and the guidance of Holy Spirit through prayer, then codified and expressed in *creedal theology*—has been adopted by the majority of practicing Christians as the fundamental doctrines of our belief system. In short, the fruit of the seven ecumenical councils is what helps keep believers and churches from flying off the God-ordained rails of biblical Christianity.

42

Soteriology

SOTERIOLOGY: *Sōtēr* is a Greek word that means "deliverer" or "rescuer," so it stands to reason that soteriology is the theological discipline focused on understanding salvation and how humanity moves from a state of deprivation to one of release or fulfillment.[1] Christian soteriology is primarily concerned with explicating how God's saving work is accomplished through Jesus Christ. It emphasizes that the story of Jesus plays a decisive role in human redemption, exploring how this narrative illuminates and transforms the reader's world and life.[2]

Several years ago I had the undeserved privilege of leading the women's retreat at a very large, very conservative church where wiggling during musical worship was less common than a barbecue-rib food truck at a vegan festival. Their constrained atmosphere was kind of like that of the fictional town in the movie *Footloose*—mind you, this is not a personal recommendation of that particular film; I watched it during a prodigal season! Anyway, after spending a day and a half with those dear women, I decided to teach on the last two psalms in the

1. John Polkinghorne, *Science and Christian Belief: Theological Reflections of a Bottom-Up Thinker* (SPCK, 1994), 198.

2. Michael Root, "The Narrative Structure of Soteriology," in *Why Narrative? Readings in Narrative Theology*, ed. Stanley Hauerwas and L. Gregory Jones (Wipf and Stock, 1997), 264.

Psalter (149 and 150) for the final session. Each of which includes directives commanding God's people to dance while praising Him (149:3; 150:4). Suffice it to say my message was received with a lot of crossed arms and very few amens, and I've never been invited back to speak at that church.

But here's the silver lining: Right after the event concluded and the crowd began to disperse, a soft-spoken woman approached me and said she was surprised that I brought up the topic of dancing in the Bible. I told her I surprised myself and admitted the topic may have been prompted by too much coffee at breakfast instead of the Holy Spirit. She laughed good-naturedly, then went on to explain how a few days before the retreat she sensed God whispering, "I want you to learn to dance with Me," during her prayer time. She continued sheepishly, "Because I'm Black, people tend to assume that I have good rhythm and like to dance, but I'm actually not much of a dancer. I was always more of a serious-minded student than a free spirit. So when God asked me to dance with Him, I initially felt self-conscious and awkward." She paused for a few seconds before smiling broadly and confessing conspiratorially, "But when you started going on about dancing this morning *in this environment*, I heard God speak to my spirit again. And this time He said to stop concentrating on my 'two left feet' and just focus on His face!"

That's the bottom line when it comes to soteriology too—it's about focusing on Jesus and what faith in Him affords us, including:

- **Justification:** being made righteous and reconciled to the one true, holy God through Jesus's sinless life and sacrificial death
- **Sanctification:** having a new identity in Jesus Christ, with the obligation and devotion to live an increasingly Jesus-shaped life according to that identity
- **Glorification:** the completion, perfection, consummation, and full realization of salvation when we meet our Lord and Savior, Jesus, face-to-face

There's an overt soteriological theme woven throughout Scripture—it's the whole point of *His*tory!—and it fairly jumps off the page in the Christmas narrative. First, consider Mary's melodic response (aka "the Magnificat") after finding out God has chosen her to give birth to the long-awaited Messiah:

> My soul glorifies the Lord
>   and my spirit rejoices in God *my Savior*,
> for he has been mindful
>   of the humble state of his servant.
> From now on all generations will call me blessed,
>   for the Mighty One has done great things for me—
>   holy is his name.
> His mercy extends to those who fear him,
>   from generation to generation.
> He has performed mighty deeds with his arm;
>   he has scattered those who are proud in their inmost thoughts.
> He has brought down rulers from their thrones
>   but has lifted up the humble.
> He has filled the hungry with good things
>   but has sent the rich away empty.
> He has helped his servant Israel,
>   remembering to be merciful
> to Abraham and his descendants forever,
>   just as he promised our ancestors. (Luke 1:46–55)

The word Mary uses for "Savior" in this praise chorus is *sōtēr* in Greek, which we've already established means "deliverer" or "rescuer." Then, when she and Joseph take baby Jesus to the temple forty days after His birth to offer a ceremonial sacrifice for their firstborn son in accordance with Mosaic law, they're greeted by a dear old fellow named Simeon. Can't you just picture his incredulous expression when they approach and Joseph asks something along the lines of, "I'm sorry to bother you, sir, but can you tell us where to go to give Yahweh a gift on behalf of our little boy?" Simeon probably took a deep breath to steady himself before reaching his gnarled hands toward the teenage mother and asking softly, "May I hold him?" To which I bet Mary nodded and handed Simeon the six-week-old Son of God! I imagine Simeon cradling the pink-cheeked Messiah for several minutes before he began to sing a song he'd written years before but had never actually sung out loud.

> Now there was a man in Jerusalem called Simeon, who was righteous and devout. He was waiting for the consolation of Israel, and the Holy Spirit was on him. It had been revealed to him by the Holy Spirit that he would not die before he had seen the Lord's Messiah. Moved by the Spirit, he went into the temple courts. When the parents brought in the child Jesus to do for him what the custom of the Law required, Simeon took him in his arms and praised God, saying [singing]:
>
> "Sovereign Lord, as you have promised,
> you may now dismiss your servant in peace.
> For my eyes have seen *your salvation*,
> which you have prepared in the sight of all nations:
> a light for revelation to the Gentiles,
> and the glory of your people Israel." (Luke 2:25–32)

Surely Mary smiled when that wrinkled saint warbled the words "your salvation" because *salvation* comes from the Greek word *sōtērion*—almost an exact replica of the lyric she composed and sang after Gabriel told her she was going to give birth to God the Son. In other words, a wide-eyed but faithful teenage mom and a wizened but still faithful octogenarian are recorded as belting the very same tune about Jesus being the *Savior* the world is longing for. That may be one too many Greek dots to connect in one setting for some, but it's an epic mic-drop moment for Bible nerds everywhere!

- **WHY *SOTERIOLOGY* MATTERS:** The red thread of redemption that points to Jesus throughout both the Old and New Testaments proves that it was *always* our heavenly Father's plan to rescue and redeem us. The canopy over human history is that there is one true God who loves His people so much that He gave His one and only Son, that whoever believes in Him shall not perish but have eternal life.

43

Spiritual Gifts

SPIRITUAL GIFTS: The word *gift* in the New Testament comes from either the Greek word *pneumatika*, which means "spirit things," or the Greek word *charismata*, which means "grace things."[1] The general sense of the term *spiritual gifts* covers all endowments of the Spirit found in the Christian experience and designed to be of service to the church.[2]

I've been in church since I was in utero and in vocational ministry or "service to the church" since I was in my early twenties. In those ecclesiastical contexts I've taken approximately 682 tests/assessments/inventories regarding what my spiritual gifts are. Okay, that's slightly exaggerative, but there is a plethora of published material regarding spiritual gifts, and new tests/assessments/inventories trend every few years, setting off a flurry of sermon series, books, blogs, and podcasts on the topic. And while the tests/assessments/inventories vary in how they determine someone's spiritual gifts as well as the number of spiritual gifts that are available for Christ followers, the primary biblical passage they're all based on is 1 Corinthians 12:

1. Jim Howard and Donald Payne, syllabus and teaching notes, Biblical and Theological Reflection on the Practice of Ministry, Denver Seminary, July 2019.

2. Ralph P. Martin, "Gifts, Spiritual," in *Anchor Yale Bible Dictionary*, vol. 2, 1016.

Now about the *gifts of the Spirit* [*pneumatikos*—"spirit things"], brothers and sisters, I do not want you to be uninformed. You know that when you were pagans, somehow or other you were influenced and led astray to mute idols. Therefore I want you to know that no one who is speaking by the Spirit of God says, "Jesus be cursed," and no one can say, "Jesus is Lord," except by the Holy Spirit.

There are different kinds of *gifts* [*charisma*—"grace"], but the same Spirit distributes them. There are different kinds of service, but the same Lord. There are different kinds of working, but in all of them and in everyone it is the same God at work.

Now to each one the manifestation of the Spirit is given for the common good. To one there is given through the Spirit a message of wisdom, to another a message of knowledge by means of the same Spirit, to another faith by the same Spirit, to another *gifts* [*charismata*—"grace things"] of healing by that one Spirit, to another miraculous powers, to another prophecy, to another distinguishing between spirits, to another speaking in different kinds of tongues, and to still another the interpretation of tongues. All these are the work of one and the same Spirit, and he distributes them to each one, just as he determines.

Just as a body, though one, has many parts, but all its many parts form one body, so it is with Christ. For we were all baptized by one Spirit so as to form one body—whether Jews or Gentiles, slave or free—and we were all given the one Spirit to drink. Even so the body is not made up of one part but of many.

Now if the foot should say, "Because I am not a hand, I do not belong to the body," it would not for that reason stop being part of the body. And if the ear should say, "Because I am not an eye, I do not belong to the body," it would not for that reason stop being part of the body. If the whole body were an eye, where would the sense of hearing be? If the whole body were an ear, where would the sense of smell be? But in fact God has placed the parts in the body, every one of them, just as he wanted them to be. If they were all one part, where would the body be? As it is, there are many parts, but one body.

The eye cannot say to the hand, "I don't need you!" And the head cannot say to the feet, "I don't need you!" On the contrary, those parts of the body

> that seem to be weaker are indispensable, and the parts that we think are less honorable we treat with special honor. And the parts that are unpresentable are treated with special modesty, while our presentable parts need no special treatment. But God has put the body together, giving greater honor to the parts that lacked it, so that there should be no division in the body, but that its parts should have equal concern for each other. If one part suffers, every part suffers with it; if one part is honored, every part rejoices with it.
>
> Now you are the body of Christ, and each one of you is a part of it. And God has placed in the church first of all apostles, second prophets, third teachers, then miracles, then *gifts* [*charismata*—"grace things"] of healing, of helping, of guidance, and of different kinds of tongues. Are all apostles? Are all prophets? Are all teachers? Do all work miracles? Do all have *gifts* [*charismata*—"grace things"] of healing? Do all speak in tongues? Do all interpret? Now eagerly desire the *greater gifts* [*megas charisma*—"greater grace"]. (vv. 1–31)

If you'll take the time to read the above passage slowly and in the accurate sociohistorical context regarding all the fussing, fighting, and jockeying for position that was going on in the first-century Corinthian church to whom this epistle was originally addressed, it becomes glaringly apparent that it's more about grace than gifts. Paul was addressing the growing schism that was threatening to divide their fellowship because those immature Christ followers presumed certain spiritual gifts were cooler than others, and they thought possessing the "cooler gifts" would allow them to occupy the highest rung of spiritual superiority in their ancient God squad.

If he'd been speaking modern English, his response would've been along the lines of: *Geez Louise! Y'all really want to know who's the "most spiritual" in this motley crew? Whoever has confessed Jesus Christ as Lord are the spiritual ones! That's the criteria. It doesn't matter if you have a bright and shiny public gift that other people like on social media or your gift is exercised quietly and privately with little to no fanfare—if you've put your hope in Jesus Christ, you're spiritual. Every single one of you has awesome Spirit things and grace things through which to bless each other and honor God!*

Despite humanity's tendency to create hierarchies of value for everything from what kind of furniture we have in our family rooms to how God shaped us to function in the church—*His family room*—Paul's point is there's no A team and B team with our Creator. We prone-to-wander people are prone to covet some spiritual gifts more than others too, but they're equally beneficial for the body of Christ, and it behooves us to remember they're not meritorious. They are instead the means through which Holy Spirit takes hold of our lives and uses us to build our communities of faith and amplify God's glory.

Remember what Paul says to Timothy, who was a young man who struggled with confidence: "Fan into flame the gift of God" (2 Tim. 1:6). What does that mean? It means the gifts are not "magic"—they're divine and we have to *lean into them with the cognizance that they need to be in tandem with the Spirit or they have no life!*

- **WHY *SPIRITUAL GIFTS* MATTER:** Because they are a distinct set of abilities sovereignly and strategically distributed by God to His children so that we can join in His kingdom purposes. Spiritual gifts bring a sense of purpose to individual believers, but they are best executed in harmony with other believers who have their own set of spiritual gifts, much like combining individual notes can create a symphony of sound. The Christian church functions best the way we see it depicted in the New Testament book of Acts—when all of those who've put their faith in Jesus are investing their spiritual gifts for His glory and the benefit of other image bearers.

44

Syncretism

■ **SYNCRETISM:** The blending or incorporation of practices, teachings, or beliefs from different religious traditions into a single system.[1] In the context of Christianity, it is often viewed as a process where Christian beliefs and practices are reshaped, either consciously or unconsciously, to reflect the dominant culture, potentially causing Christianity to lose its distinctiveness.[2]

My first trip to Haiti was a sensory overload, to put it mildly. I'd traveled there to meet a toddler named Missy whose mother had just passed away. Through a miraculous connection, her caregivers had asked if I'd be willing to adopt her because there was no one in her country who had the capacity to care for her unique medical needs. So I was about to meet the precious, traumatized toddler I hoped would one day become my daughter. When our flight (I traveled with several friends from Nashville) from Miami landed in Port-au-Prince, my mind and heart were filled with an amalgamation of excitement, apprehension, faith, anxiety, and hope. And, of course, our arrival did nothing to calm my

1. Arthur G. Patzia and Anthony J. Petrotta, *Pocket Dictionary of Biblical Studies*, The IVP Pocket Reference Series (IVP Academic, 2002), under "syncretism."

2. KimSon Nguyen, *Cultural Integration and the Gospel in Vietnamese Mission Theology: A Paradigm Shift* (Langham Monographs, 2019), 56–57.

nerves because bag claim was teeming with entrepreneurial and aggressive young men vying for the chance to "help" us with our luggage. By the time I'd made it through the chaos of customs, and scrambled out into the oppressive, triple-digit heat, my peace was hovering near empty.

But then I felt a surge of calm joy when we loaded onto the school bus that was transporting us to Missy's village because I noticed we were surrounded by cabs (they're called "tap-taps" in Haiti and are mostly older-model pickup trucks or minivans that have been stripped of the seats so as to cram as many passengers on board as possible) covered with brightly painted images of Jesus, crosses, and lots of other Christian symbols. When I pointed out the evangelistic motorcade to my hostess, she chuckled good-naturedly and said, "Those aren't actually 'Christian' because all those other images you see painted on the tap-taps are voodoo symbols—the Jesus portraits are just to 'cover their bases,' kind of like carrying a four-leaf clover in your pocket for good luck!"

Syncretism is relatively easy to spot when it's overt, such as when the hood of a pickup truck is garishly painted with a picture of Jesus adjacent to a serpent deity. But syncretism can also be dangerously subtle. Paul addressed one such case when young Christians in Colossae (now modern Turkey) were getting hoodwinked by heretics who were poisoning the purity of the gospel of Jesus Christ with a bunch of nonsense but were shrewdly making their arguments sound just "Jesus-y" enough to be palatable:

> I want you to know how hard I am contending for you and for those at Laodicea, and for all who have not met me personally. *My goal is that they may be encouraged in heart and united in love, so that they may have the full riches of complete understanding, in order that they may know the mystery of God, namely, Christ, in whom are hidden all the treasures of wisdom and knowledge. I tell you this so that no one may deceive you by fine-sounding arguments.* For though I am absent from you in body, I am present with you in spirit and delight to see how disciplined you are and how firm your faith in Christ is.

> So then, just as you received Christ Jesus as Lord, continue to live your lives in him, rooted and built up in him, strengthened in the faith as you were taught, and overflowing with thankfulness.
>
> *See to it that no one takes you captive through hollow and deceptive philosophy, which depends on human tradition and the elemental spiritual forces of this world rather than on Christ.* (Col. 2:1–8)

The first Christian church at Colossae was a young church when Paul wrote them this letter while he was incarcerated (which is why Colossians is sometimes referred to as a "prison epistle"). It was founded by an unlikely pastor named Epaphras, who got saved when he was on a business trip in Ephesus and heard Paul preach. Epaphras came home to Colossae on fire for Christ and started a house church, which grew by leaps and bounds for several years—until a few false teachers threatened to hijack the congregation of baby believers with "fine-sounding arguments," "hollow and deceptive philosophies," and "human traditions" that could loosely be described as Jewish-Hellenistic syncretism.

The CliffsNotes of their deceptive—albeit sort of "Jesus-y" sounding—messaging were:

- Jesus was a lower intermediary or an "appearance" of God.
- Humans were a divine spark imprisoned in an evil, material body.
- Salvation meant freedom from our evil human bodies.
- The way of salvation could be found through asceticism and angel worship.
- Morality was achieved through denying one's needs, drives, and desires.
- True religion was subjective and speculative.
- Angels could be used as a kind of spiritual ladder to access God.

As off-key as those beliefs should sound to a Christ follower, they initially sounded legitimate to the young Jewish and Gentile Christians in Colossae.

The Jewish believers related to the rigid, legalistic demands of this syncretistic messaging because it reminded them of Old Testament law. And the Gentile believers felt comfortable conjoining angel worship with faith in Jesus because the paganism they'd grown up with was pluralistic and mystical too. The Colossae heresy had just enough familiar spiritual semantics and rituals to ring true. Which is why the rest of Paul's letter to the Colossians reads like God's Little Instruction Book, because he clarifies the theological framework of Christianity with great precision. He makes the gospel "guardrails" high enough so that those dear, albeit immature, Christ followers in Colossae won't go off course again.

It's important to note that Paul doesn't trample potential cultural barriers but instead humbly and wisely builds bridges throughout his ministry. In Acts 13:13–43, he reveals he's a master of Old Testament history and exposition, thereby earning the respect of Jewish leaders and building a bridge for an open conversation about Jesus. But he doesn't recite the Torah in Acts 17:16–34 when he's hanging out with Greeks in Athens. Instead, he recites from a poem originally dedicated to Zeus, thereby illustrating his comprehension of the pantheon of gods they believe in, and builds another bridge for an open conversation about Jesus. In both settings, Paul finds creative ways to connect with distinctly different people groups. And while his *mechanics* of exposition differ, he doesn't change the core *message* about how salvation comes solely through faith in Jesus Christ. This is the critical difference between *contextualization,* which can lead to honest conversations about the gospel, and *capitulation,* which can lead to syncretism and unbelief.

- **WHY *SYNCRETISM* MATTERS:** We're living in a world where it's becoming increasingly tempting to tailor our beliefs—consciously or subconsciously—to be synergistic with culture so we won't be misunderstood or canceled. However, the Bible reminds us that *this world* is not our home (Heb. 13:14–16). Furthermore, as Christ followers, we'll always be aliens and strangers here because the foundation of our belief system is that Jesus is not *a way* to be reconciled with God; He's *the only way* (see John 14:6), and that truth is simply not compatible with syncretism.

45

Teleological Arc

TELEOLOGICAL ARC: The word *teleological* comes from two Greek root words, *telos*, which means "end" or "purpose," and *logos*, which means "word," "speech," "reason," or "principle." Therefore, the concept of a teleological arc refers to a purposeful trajectory or direction in history, theology, or narrative that moves toward a specific end or goal.[1]

In Christian thought, a general teleological arc refers to God's sovereign plan and design and provides a framework for understanding redemptive history from Genesis to Revelation. In short, it connects the dots between *creation* (see Gen. 1) and *covenant* (see Gen. 9:8–17; Matt. 26:27–28; Heb. 6:13–19), and ultimately to the *culmination* John describes in the caboose of this divine love story we call the Bible:

> And I heard a loud voice from the throne saying, "*Look! God's dwelling place is now among the people, and he will dwell with them. They will be his people, and God himself will be with them and be their God.* 'He will wipe every tear from

1. J. de Waal Dryden, *A Hermeneutic of Wisdom: Recovering the Formative Agency of Scripture* (Baker Academic, 2018), 127–28.

> their eyes. There will be no more death' or mourning or crying or pain, for the old order of things has passed away." (Rev. 21:3–4)

Our Christian Bible isn't a collection of disconnected essays about a faraway deity by various authors. It is instead a miraculous metanarrative—a grand story—of God's unconditional, redemptive love for humanity. God's Word is infinitely more than a plumb line through which we establish a system of ethical behavior and form our theological beliefs; it's how we frame the chapters of our lives—including the painful, disappointing, and even seemingly random ones—as well as the world around us. Dr. Eugene Peterson explains it like this:

> The Bible is basically and overall a narrative, an immense, sprawling, capacious narrative. . . . And it is a vast, over-reaching, all-encompassing story—a meta-story. . . . None of us is the leading character in the story of our lives. God is the larger context and plot in which all our stories find themselves.[2]

Case in point: My first foray into teaching the Bible was in high school when my best friend, Cindy, and I started a weekly study through the Fellowship of Christian Athletes. We were wildly enthusiastic about sharing the gospel and often long-winded in our exegesis, but it was a great adventure. And it's in that context that I first thought about adoption because one semester we decided to focus on the theme of adoption in Scripture and were so impacted that we both soberly vowed to adopt orphaned children when we grew up and got married. Cindy married soon after graduating from college, and not long afterward she and Peter adopted two children.

Meanwhile, I was one of those "always the bridesmaid, never the bride" kinds of girls. I threw myself into five years in youth ministry, followed by a six-year stint at a mostly wonderful ministry in Colorado where I had to wear

2. Eugene Peterson, "Living into God's Story," presented at the Laity Lodge Retreat, October 11, 1996, https://missionworldview.com/wp-content/uploads/2020/06/ea8a85_f728f22e39d8426e9e35f0ce85e0f4e2.pdf.

pantyhose and couldn't wear open-toed shoes because someone had convinced the leadership team that the line between a woman's big toe and second toe resembled cleavage and could cause men to have lustful thoughts. (Even back then, when I confused godly submission with the subjugation of women, I couldn't help wondering how they were connecting sanctification with confining one's legs in nylon sheaths, much less how some dude's sexual sin could be blamed on my sandals.) Alas, I sacrificed a large part of my thirties to an uncomfortable yet chaste fog.

Shortly before turning forty, I moved to Nashville to work on a church staff and attend seminary, and a year or so later I attended what proved to be a life-changing breakout session at a women's conference. I chose that particular breakout session because of the emphasis on missions, so I was thrown off guard when the facilitator began talking about adoption. She shared statistics that proved there were over 147 million orphans in the world at that time, many of whom were languishing in developing countries with little hope of surviving infancy because of easily preventable diseases like malaria, cholera, and tuberculosis, as well as widespread malnutrition. Then she quoted that familiar verse in James about how taking care of widows and orphans is our responsibility as Christ followers, after which she paused for a long moment—taking the time to look many of us directly in the eyes—before asking intently, "What are *you* doing about it?"

I can still remember the conviction that reverberated through the room and through my spirit that Saturday afternoon twenty years ago. I wasn't sure how to answer her question because as a forty-year-old single woman from a conservative theological background, I wasn't sure I was even *allowed* to adopt a child even though I'd vowed to do so when I was in high school and assumed I'd get married right after I graduated from college. I mean, good night, I'd just begun to exercise the liberty of leaving the house without pantyhose! But I couldn't shake the feeling that God was again calling me to do *something* about orphans.

It took seven more years before I had enough faith to say yes. And I experienced two failed adoption attempts—one at the eleventh hour, just a few days before I was supposed to bring the baby home from the hospital. A few weeks after that devastating loss, an old friend I hadn't seen or talked to in years called and said she'd just returned home from a medical mission trip to Haiti, and while she was there, one of the young moms in the village she was visiting died, leaving behind a very sick two-and-a-half-year-old daughter named Missy. She explained that if someone—really, *anyone*—didn't step into Missy's story and make sure she got the medicine and care she was desperate for, the doctors in Port-au-Prince predicted she'd die within two months. Then she said, "Lisa, when the doctor asked if we knew anyone who might take a chance on Missy, the Holy Spirit whispered, 'Lisa Harper is supposed to be that little girl's mama.' I know you're heartbroken right now, but I wonder if you'd still be willing to pray about starting the adoption process with her."

I replied, "Nope. I've been praying about this for years, Michelle . . . go ahead and sign me up."

Two years later, on April 14, 2014, I brought my daughter, Melissa Price Harper, home from Haiti. If you'd told me in 1981—when I was a seventeen-year-old senior in high school—that my vow to adopt would take thirty-three years to fulfill, I probably would've retracted the promise. But now when I look back over those three-plus decades of delay through the miraculous lens of motherhood, I can see the common denominator of God's mercy in every single moment. The priceless gift of parenthood has provided irrefutable proof that God always had a purpose and a plan for Missy and me. My belief in a teleological arc hasn't just informed my eschatology (although the two are closely related); it has greatly increased my security in our Redeemer's sovereignty.

Devotees of all three major world religions—Judaism, Islam, and Christianity—also believe there is a divine purpose and plan for our lives. However, Christianity is the only belief system in which the centerpiece of God's agenda was to become like us and sacrifice Himself on a cross to save us. Our teleological arc is the only divine blueprint that's painstakingly written out in the precious blood of the Lamb of God.

- **WHY *TELEOLOGICAL ARC* MATTERS:** Because it provides the framework for understanding the ultimate meaning of life. In the same way the concept of telos refers to the purpose and function of an object, such as how a boat's telos is to carry people and/or products across water, so the teleological arc of Christianity reveals the purpose of life, and the function of humanity exists under God's master plan to redeem His image bearers from our sinful state and reconcile us back into a right relationship with Him.

46

Theodicy

■ **THEODICY:** A response to the problem of evil in the world that attempts logically, relevantly, and consistently to defend God as simultaneously omnipotent, all-loving, and just despite the reality of evil.[1]

A German philosopher and mathematician named Gottfried Leibniz coined the term *theodicy* almost three hundred years ago by combining two Greek words—*theos,* which refers to God, and *dikē,* which is the name of the Greek goddess of justice and therefore represents a sense of moral order. Yet while that theological term is a mere three centuries old, people have been trying to reconcile the hard edges of life against the backdrop of a benevolent God for much, much longer. *If God is such a good God, why is life filled with evil, suffering, and hardship?* is not a remotely modern dilemma.

Historians have discovered texts dating as far back as 403 BC in which ancient philosophers wrestled with the idea of a deity/deities who were indifferent or even hostile when "bad" things happened to "good" people. And of course, it's not just unbelievers who've questioned how divine providence could be braided with mercy, given the prevalence of pain and evil in the world. Even Abraham,

1. Grenz, Guretzki, and Nordling, *Pocket Dictionary of Theological Terms,* under "theodicy."

the father of our three major world religions—Judaism, Islam, and Christianity—questioned God's absolute goodness when he bargained with Him on behalf of the citizens of Sodom, among whom Abraham assumed were at least fifty "good guys."

> Then Abraham approached him and said: "*Will you sweep away the righteous with the wicked? What if there are fifty righteous people in the city? Will you really sweep it away and not spare the place for the sake of the fifty righteous people in it? Far be it from you to do such a thing—to kill the righteous with the wicked, treating the righteous and the wicked alike. Far be it from you! Will not the Judge of all the earth do right?*"
>
> The LORD said, "If I find fifty righteous people in the city of Sodom, I will spare the whole place for their sake." (Gen. 18:23–26)

And the inauspicious list goes on. Moses, Gideon, Habakkuk, Jonah, King David, Peter, Paul, and many other saints throughout Scripture had weak moments when their theodicy deficiencies were exposed. Thankfully our Creator Redeemer is rich in compassion and slow to anger (see Ps. 145:8), and He wove a knot at the end of their ropes and pulled them back to the solid ground of faith. But when it comes to Bible characters being towed back to the beach of belief, I must confess Job is my all-time favorite. Because while he's still reeling from horrific trauma that would cause even the most seasoned therapist to flinch, he gets it. Thousands of years before that German math whiz coined the term, Job modeled theodicy:

> Then Job replied to the LORD:
>
> "I know that you can do all things;
> no purpose of yours can be thwarted.
> You asked, 'Who is this that obscures my plans without knowledge?'
> *Surely I spoke of things I did not understand,*
> *things too wonderful for me to know.*

> "You said, 'Listen now, and I will speak;
> I will question you,
> and you shall answer me.'
> *My ears had heard of you*
> *but now my eyes have seen you.*" (Job 42:1–5)

Job's belief in God's absolute goodness has rightly echoed down through Judeo-Christian history because of how he praised God's faithfulness *before* God healed his broken heart. And while it's heartwarming to read the rest of chapter 42, which details how his health, wealth, and family were restored, I think the most miraculous aspect of Job's story is that getting his life back wasn't a prerequisite for him to plant his trust firmly in the faithfulness of God. He *still* couldn't see around the corner of his circumstances when he exclaimed, "My ears had heard of you, but *now* my eyes have seen *you*" (v. 5). In other words, *No matter what happens in the future, I'm okay as long as You're with me, Father.*

The pre-restorative timing of Job's renewed faith is a profound illustration of *theodicy*. Because getting the life we always hoped for isn't the true source of our peace, contentment, and joy. It is instead our Savior's palpable presence in the seasons *we didn't hope for* that gives us peace beyond our understanding and contentment regardless of our circumstances. The steadfast presence and immutable love of God are the reasons we can radiate genuine joy—even when our eyes are filled with tears.

■ **WHY *THEODICY* MATTERS:** Because dealing honestly, wisely, and compassionately with human pain is an integral part of our job description as followers of Jesus Christ. No one gets through this life unscathed. Everyone deals with pain and suffering at some level, and since God's second most important command is to love our neighbors as we love ourselves, it behooves us to learn how to better comfort and empathize with our neighbors who ache and grieve and can't help but wonder how a good and all-powerful God can coexist with all the evil and suffering in our world.

47

Theological Anthropology

THEOLOGICAL ANTHROPOLOGY: Loosely refers to the way in which our knowledge of who God is and how He reveals Himself through His Spirit and His Word has evolved over the course of human history. Theological anthropology is a specific domain of studying Scripture and personhood. Theological realism is that we hold on to what we know to be true of God but are willing to grow in the area of understanding better who we are in light of who God is.[1]

For instance, imago Dei—the biblical truism that humans are made in the *image of God*—is a concept first used in Genesis 1:26–27. It's an overt concept throughout that entire first chapter of Holy Writ because God describes human beings as "*very* good" (v. 31) after describing previous tactile created order—from moons to mangoes—as simply "good" (see vv. 3–25). In other words, there's something *uniquely valuable* about humans from our heavenly Father's perspective.

Yet while the creation account in Genesis is riddled with the idea of imago Dei—making it what some of my seminary professors call a "load-bearing wall"

1. Jim Howard and Donald Payne, syllabus and teaching notes, Biblical and Theological Reflection on the Practice of Ministry, Denver Seminary, July 2019.

of Christian orthodoxy—this concept as a whole isn't really picked up again until Paul's writing in the New Testament. And by then, the concept has a bit more color, nuance, and heft. Because over the course of thousands of years of redemptive history (the story of redemption moves *forward* through the pages of Scripture—it is *not* a stagnant text), God's people continued to wrestle with what it meant to be created in His image.

They began to ask questions like, *If the image of God is what gives humans our unique dignity, then what happens when a person loses their rationality because of a brain tumor or a traumatic brain injury?* You can almost imagine rabbis and pastors and evangelists throughout the years popping up from their hunched position of perusing the Scriptures and smacking themselves in the forehead when they have an aha moment like, *Oh, wow, obviously our inherent value as image bearers can't be based solely on our mental acuity!*

The more God's people pondered what it meant for us to be made in His image, the more facets of that metaphorical divine diamond that came to light. The anthropological progression of theology in the Christian church grew to encompass components like:

- **Rationality:** When our minds are renewed by the Spirit of God and the Word of God, they have the capacity for Christoformity: "The person with the Spirit makes judgments about all things, but such a person is not subject to merely human judgments, for 'Who has known the mind of the Lord so as to instruct him?' But *we have the mind of Christ*" (1 Cor. 2:15–16).
- **Relationships:** When we love others well, we have the capacity to remind people of Jesus's unconditional love: "A new command I give you: Love one another. As I have loved you, so you must love one another. *By this everyone will know that you are my disciples, if you love one another*" (John 13:34–35).

- **Functionality:** When we operate redemptively in society, we have the capacity to reflect the unity and grace of our trinitarian God: "All the believers were together and had everything in common. They sold property and possessions to give to anyone who had need. Every day they continued to meet together in the temple courts. They broke bread in their homes and ate together with glad and sincere hearts, praising God and enjoying the favor of all the people. And the Lord added to their number daily those who were being saved" (Acts 2:44–47).

Theological anthropology doesn't alter biblical truth; it elucidates it—it makes it clearer. It's like what happened when I was scrolling the aisles of Amazon late one night when I couldn't sleep and bought a pair of binoculars on sale because the ad mentioned that they were good for bird-watching. While I'm not a true bird aficionado, I'm an ardent fan of the hummingbirds that frequent our five-acre farmette here in Middle Tennessee. In fact, I've intentionally planted perennials with bright red and orange blooms to attract them, plus I have enough feeders hanging around the outside of our log home to fatten up a whole flock. I didn't think I could be more fascinated by those shy sugar-water addicts, but the binoculars have turned my appreciation up several notches. Of course, those wee critters were beautiful to behold before I could see them magnified, but now I can admire the gorgeous blue and green hues in their individual feathers, I can see how perfectly shaped their long beaks are for sipping nectar from even the most petite flower, and I can even watch their tiny heads tilt warily toward me while they're sipping from a feeder to make sure I'm a friend and not a foe.

Biblical truths *don't* change—they are as relevant, life-giving, and timeless now as they were when God breathed them—but as redemptive history moves forward, toward the *consummation of glory* (when we will step into heaven and see Him face-to-face), our capacity to understand and appreciate them does.

- **WHY *THEOLOGICAL ANTHROPOLOGY* MATTERS:** Because it's kind of like the focus knob on a powerful telescope—it gives us a framework within which to view ourselves as creatures whom God has made, rescued, redeemed, and is currently sanctifying. Then, as time passes, theological anthropology elucidates the image of ourselves as God's beloved, so our understanding of who He is and who He's called us to be becomes more well-defined, which matures our faith and deepens our commitment to become more like Jesus as we await His Parousia.

48

Theology

■ **THEOLOGY:** "The 'science of God.' Among the Greek Fathers it comes to have two specific references: it can denote either the doctrine of the Trinity (i.e., of God's being, as opposed to his dealings with the created order), or it can mean prayer (as it is only in prayer that God is truly known). Later it came to mean the science of the Divinely revealed religious truths. Its theme is the Being and Nature of God and His creatures and the whole complex of the Divine dispensation from the Fall of Adam to the Redemption through Christ and its mediation to men by His Church, including the so-called natural truths of God, the soul, the moral law, etc., which are accessible to mere reason. Its purpose is the investigation of the contents of belief by means of reason enlightened by faith (*fides quaerens intellectum*) and the promotion of its deeper understanding. In the course of time theology has developed into several branches, among them dogmatic, historical, and practical theology. The methods of classification of the sub-disciplines, however, fluctuate in different theological systems."[1]

I know, I know, that's a long, complicated-sounding definition with lots of fifty-dollar seminary words. But don't worry, we're about to responsibly truncate

1. F. L. Cross and Elizabeth A. Livingstone, eds., *The Oxford Dictionary of the Christian Church*, 3rd ed. (Oxford University Press, 2005), under "theology."

and translate it into something a bit more user friendly! The original Greek root words that the English word *theology* is translated from are *theos,* which refers to God, and *logos* or *logia,* which refer to utterances, sayings, or words. Therefore, the basic definition of *theology* is "conversations about God." And conversation implies relationship, right? Furthermore, genuine relationships framed in the context of conversation are not simply transactional; they're personal. They require some measure of mental energy and emotional engagement. They affect our minds and our hearts. When we really ponder the essential meaning of the term *theology,* it becomes clear that it's not merely about learning—accruing facts *about God*—instead it's about living in an increasingly more intimate relationship *with God.*

I so appreciate the way German theologian Helmut Thielicke framed theology: "A theological thought can breathe only in the atmosphere of dialogue with God."[2] Another one of my favorite quotes that's often attributed to Thielicke (but is likely a summation taken from his published material) is "Unless a theology works at the margins of life, it's not worth anything even if it makes sense at the easy center."[3] It emphasizes the fact that theology is more practical than it is pristine and purely academic. In other words, it's not just for seminary professors and pastors; the pursuit of deep, biblically informed theology is also for regular folks like us who are doing our best to live faithful, Jesus-shaped lives while navigating the rapture and rupture of real life.

My dear friend Christine Caine and I used to go round and round about this because whenever I'd use some theological term, she'd say, "Quit using all those big words, Lease; I am *not* a theologian." To which I'd retort, "Oh yes you *are* a theologian, Chris, because you talk with and about God all the time!" She eventually came around to my line of reasoning (it's one of the only disagreements I've ever won with Chris because she is one smart cookie!) that

2. Helmut Thielicke, *A Little Exercise for Young Theologians* (Eerdmans, 1962), 34.

3. Jim Howard and Donald Payne, syllabus and teaching notes, Biblical and Theological Reflection on the Practice of Ministry, Denver Seminary, July 2019.

technically everyone's a theologian because pretty much everyone has conversations about God (at least in their own head). However, unless you frame your thoughts and conversations by how God reveals Himself through the Holy Scriptures and the Holy Spirit, you run the risk of being a wackadoodle theologian ruled by your own preferences and opinions.

Here's the deal: *Everyone's* invited to dive into the deep, faith-fertilizing waters of biblically sound theology. It's so much more than a system to organize our thoughts about God and so much better than a belief system to modify our behavior and ensure we won't say words that aren't in the Bible when we're stuck in bad traffic. It's an incredibly rewarding adventure that will lead us further and further into the unconditional love of the one true God.

- **WHY *THEOLOGY* MATTERS:** Because in light of the basic definition of *theology*—"conversations about God"—it's not academic subject matter reserved for pastors and seminary students; *theology* encompasses the meaning of life itself! It's how we understand, communicate, and live out everything we know to be true about God, His unconditional love for us, and the kingdom purposes He invites us to take part in.

49

Theopneustos

THEOPNEUSTOS: Built from the Greek root words *theos,* which refers to God, and *pneō,* which means "to blow" or "to breathe out." *Theopneustos* occurs only once in the Bible (2 Tim. 3:16), and when Paul applied this term to Scripture, he introduced an unusual category for texts, which were not usually thought of as having religious authority in the Hellenistic world.[1]

Every spring and summer throughout high school and most of college I worked as a lifeguard. When I wasn't patrolling the beach at Lake Swan Camp, I was corralling slippery kids at Sanford Bath and Tennis Club or overseeing sunburned tourists at Wekiwa Springs State Park. However, for all the days spent twirling a whistle back and forth around my finger while wearing a red bathing suit, I don't think I ever truly saved anyone's life.

I had lots of so-called rescues, but they usually consisted of pulling a panicky dog-paddler out of the deep end or assisting a fatigued swimmer who thought they couldn't make it back to shore. There was one close call when I rushed toward the screams of a non-petite, panic-stricken woman wedged in an inner tube. However, all I had to do was slather her in suntan oil, and she popped right out—crisis averted.

1. Michael Harding, "Preserved for Proclamation and Transformation," in Williams and Shaylor, *God's Word in Our Hands,* 339–40.

In contrast to my ho-hum lifeguarding career, when the psalmist exclaims, "I will never forget your precepts, *for by them you have preserved my life*" (Ps. 119:93), he's not implying the Bible is standing around looking bored, hoping one of us will get in over our heads so it can cool off. Nor is God's Word simply a raft to flop onto when we get a little winded. Scripture isn't a lifeguard; it's a *lifesaver*. Without its guidance, we would surely be swept away by the undertow of our own bad choices, faulty reasoning, and prejudiced decisions. Left to our own devices, we would all get hopelessly stuck in some kind of situational inner tube. If we don't cling to the parameters and promises in this love letter written to us by our heavenly Father, the peace and joy in our hearts will sputter and flail and eventually sink to the bottom. We simply can't swim successfully in the sea of life without God's counsel.

Unfortunately, much like the tagline of the old comic Rodney Dangerfield, I think the Bible "doesn't get much respect" and may be one of the most misunderstood books in history. Many dismiss it as a textbook filled with facts to memorize about God or a rule book filled with punitive decrees about things like not drinking or dancing or simply as a collection of tall tales like Aesop's Fables. But the Bible isn't a textbook or a rule book or a collection of benign morality tales—at its core, the Bible is a divine *love story*. From cover to cover, it describes the unconditional love our Creator and Redeemer has for us, His very messy, mistake-prone people.

And while our Creator Redeemer *inspired* human "secretaries" to write His words down, He's the one who *expired* them—He *breathed* these life-giving, life-changing promises and parameters into existence. Which is proved by the unique Greek term *theopneustos* Paul used in his second letter to his disciple Timothy to describe Scripture's supernatural genesis:

> *All Scripture is God-breathed* and is useful for teaching, rebuking, correcting and training in righteousness, so that the servant of God may be thoroughly equipped for every good work. (2 Tim. 3:16–17)

The uniqueness of divine authorship is evidenced by the term itself because *theopneustos* is a hapax legomenon, which is another fancy word that means it's only used once in a corpus of literature. *Theopneustos*—"God-breathed"—is only used to describe *one book*, the Christian Bible, which dates all the way back to when God handed Moses the beginning of this sacred, redemptive story on top of a mountain after He delivered the Israelites out of captivity in Egypt:

> When he finished speaking with him on Mount Sinai, *he gave Moses two tablets of Testimony*, slabs of stone, written with the finger of God. (Exod. 31:18 MSG)

Over the next fifteen hundred years, forty-some believers were inspired by the Holy Spirit to inscribe the rest of the Holy Writ. Then God commissioned still others to translate those original biblical texts—which were written in Hebrew, Greek, and Aramaic—into other languages, beginning with Latin, then English, and so on. To date, the entire Bible has been translated into almost eight hundred languages, the New Testament has been translated into almost two thousand different languages, and at least one book of the Bible has been translated into around four thousand of the seven-thousand-plus known languages in the world.[2]

Our Creator Redeemer commissioned still others to organize the Holy Scriptures into a single collated book (formally known as the canon of Scripture—*canon* means "norm" or "rule of faith") that we can now hold in our hands (or peruse on our computers, e-readers, and smartphones). The complete Old and New Testament canon was generally agreed upon in the mid-fourth century, as evidenced by a list written by ancient church father Athanasius in AD 367. Over the next century several ecumenical councils—formal meetings of ancient church leaders—were convened to establish the theological doctrines of our Christian belief system, as well as to formally ratify the biblical canon.

2. "Global Scripture Access," Wycliffe Global Alliance, August 2025, https://wycliffe.net/global-scripture-access/.

Mind you, there was some bickering among saints following the Protestant Reformation in the sixteenth century regarding the inclusion of certain books in the Bible, and as a result there is a variance in the number of books in Protestant Bibles, Catholic Bibles, and Eastern Orthodox Bibles. Sixty-six books are included in the Protestant Bible. However, if you're a member of the Catholic church, your Bible is heftier because it includes a section called the deuterocanonical books, which is also known as the Apocrypha. And if you're a member of the Eastern Orthodox church, your Bible comprises the Septuagint—which is the Greek translation of the Old Testament—as well as the Protestant version of the New Testament *and* the deuterocanonical books. The great news is that one of these versions of the Christian Bible is read by approximately six billion people on a regular basis!

- **WHY *THEOPNEUSTOS* MATTERS:** Scripture's legitimacy isn't based on the perspective, opinion, and preference of God's people—this divine love letter was authored by *Him*. Therefore, our Bible isn't simply a collection of inspirational words to memorize or pull memes from for social media. And it's certainly not some religious op-ed with which we can manipulate and marginalize other image bearers. Instead, everything we read on the thin pages of this miraculous, God-breathed book must be understood, interpreted, and applied under the canopy of His absolute authority and His unconditional love.

50

The Trinity

THE TRINITY: A fundamental Christian doctrine that describes God as one being existing eternally in three persons: Father, Son, and Holy Spirit.[1] While the term *Trinity* itself does not appear in the Bible, the concept is rooted in both Old and New Testament Scriptures.[2]

Several years ago, a friend of mine overheard her preschooler having a very serious discussion about matters of faith with another preschooler at the park. Her little girl listened patiently and respectfully to the other five-year-old explaining what religion her family belonged to and how they didn't go to church on Sundays because they went to a totally different kind of "temple," and my friend found herself thinking, *Wow, I'm so glad my daughter's showing respect to this other little peanut as one of God's image bearers even though their family aren't Christ followers*, at which point her baby girl sighed loudly and proclaimed earnestly, "Well, I think our God is *more better* than yours because He's a triple!"

Although I don't advocate accosting strangers in public spaces with doctrinal absolutes, I can't think of a much clearer nod to trinitarian theology than *God*

1. Michael S. Heiser, *What Does God Want?* (Blind Spot Press, 2018), 98.
2. D. Larry Gregg, "Trinity," in *Eerdmans Dictionary of the Bible*, ed. David Noel Freedman, Allen C. Myers, and Astrid B. Beck (Eerdmans, 2000), 1336.

is more better because He's a triple! But it did sound a bit more appropriate and erudite when Saint Augustine described our Creator Redeemer (the "Christian God") as "the only One who exists in a perfect community unto Himself."[3] Augustine went on to further explain that the Trinity was not extraneous or supplementary to our Christian faith but the very heart of the gospel.

Modern theological scholar Dr. Kevin Vanhoozer puts it like this: "The integrity of the gospel is fatally compromised if either the Son or the Spirit is not fully God. If the Son were not God, he could neither reveal the Father nor atone for our sin. If the Spirit were not God, he could unite us neither to the Father and Son nor one another. The Gospel then, requires a triune God."[4]

The essential doctrine of the Trinity came as a result of the very first gathering of Christian leaders at the Council of Nicaea in AD 325 and is clearly expressed in the spiritual "manifesto" that came out of that inaugural ecumenical convention, the Nicene Creed. (The Nicene Creed is now more accurately known as the Niceno-Constantinopolitan Creed because it was revised at the Council of Constantinople in 381, and most modern Christ followers—apart from those in the Eastern Orthodox tradition—recite the second version. More details on this formational creed and the councils that drafted and edited it can be found in the chapters on Creedal Theology and the Seven Ecumenical Councils.)

Of course, the theological truism of the Trinity wasn't merely an epiphany that occurred to those saints who gathered in the ancient city of Nicaea. (Nicaea was named after *Nike*, the Greek goddess of victory,[5] and so was the global athletic brand Nike, so the next time we see one of those swooshes, let's make a pact to remember the Trinity!) It had already been percolating in the minds of early church fathers for centuries. Over a hundred years before the Nicene Creed was drafted, a godly brainiac named Tertullian (AD 160–220) affirmed

3. Augustine of Hippo, *De Trinitate*.

4. Kevin J. Vanhoozer, *Drama of Doctrine: A Canonical Linguistic Approach to Christian Theology* (Westminster John Knox, 2005), 43.

5. Litfin, *Story of the Trinity*, 120.

that the Godhead consisted of one substance/*substantia* with three distinct persons/*personae*, resulting in a "unity in Trinity."[6]

Plus, not only can we find the truism of the Trinity at the beginning of biblically orthodox theology, we can find it at the beginning of biblical history because there's a Holy Spirit shout-out in the opening line of this magnificent, mercy-riddled metanarrative called the Bible:

> In the beginning God created the heavens and the earth. Now the earth was formless and empty, darkness was over the surface of the deep, and *the Spirit of God was hovering* over the waters. (Gen. 1:1–2)

Then there's another overt trinitarian wink in the same first chapter of our redemption story when Moses explains how God made humanity in His image:

> Then God said, "*Let us* make mankind in our image, *in our* likeness, so that they may rule over the fish in the sea and the birds in the sky, over the livestock and all the wild animals, and over all the creatures that move along the ground."
>
> So God created mankind in his own image,
> in the image of God he created them;
> male and female he created them. (vv. 26–27)

In other words, God the Father, God the Son, and God the Spirit are the perfect "us"! They're perfectly connected, perfectly harmonious, perfectly balanced. Their symbiosis is supernatural, all sufficient, and self-sustaining.

Of course, there are some passages where the Trinity is more implied than explicit, like the "fourth man" in the fiery furnace with Shadrach, Meshach, and Abednego, whom ancient theologian Justin Martyr insisted was

6. Tertullian, Prax. 2.

Christophany—a visible appearance of preincarnate Jesus. But the perfectly cohesive, compassionate communion of the Trinity is evidenced throughout biblical narrative, such as when Job proclaims, "My *Redeemer* lives," and uses a Hebrew word for the Messiah, *go'al,* which is a clear reference to Jesus!

> I know that *my redeemer* lives, and that in the end he will stand on the earth. (Job 19:25)

And my favorite New Testament trinitarian narrative takes place when Johnny B. baptizes Jesus in the Jordan River:

> As soon as Jesus was baptized, he went up out of the water. At that moment heaven was opened, and he saw the *Spirit of God* descending like a dove and alighting on him. And *a voice from heaven said,* "This is my Son, whom I love; with him I am well pleased." (Matt. 3:16–17)

God the Spirit appears in the form of a dove, flapping its wings in a celebratory manner (one has to wonder if this is the genesis of a phenomenon now called "the wave" practiced by sporting fans and concertgoers around the world), eventually coming to land on Jesus. After which God the Father effectively bellows from glory, "That's my SON!"

- **WHY *THE TRINITY* MATTERS:** Our Creator Redeemer doesn't just mandate community, He models it! His trinitarian nature points to the embodied promise of the gospel of Jesus Christ—how lonely sinners like us can be woven into the family of God.

ACKNOWLEDGMENTS

I had the undeserved privilege of learning from many brilliant Bible scholars and theologians at both Denver Seminary and Houston Theological Seminary during my doctoral studies from 2019 to 2026. Most of the material in this book was gleaned from their collective wisdom. I'm also indebted to Rachel McRae, my boss at Baker Publishing Group, and my oh-so-patient-and-gifted editor Kristin Adkinson, who combed through every single word of this project and had to fix more than a few along the way!

ABOUT THE AUTHOR

Rarely are the terms *hilarious storyteller* and *theological scholar* used in the same sentence, much less to describe the same person—but then again, Lisa Harper is anything but stereotypical! She's been lauded as a compelling communicator whose writing and speaking emphasize that accruing knowledge about God pales next to a real and intimate relationship with Jesus. Her style combines sound biblical exposition and exegesis with engaging anecdotes and comedic wit.

Pastor Max Lucado calls Lisa one of the "best Bible tour guides around," and author/actress Priscilla Evans Shirer adds, "Her God-given ability to not merely teach the Word but package it in a way that stirs the heart and calls to action is incomparable. When she speaks, ears perk up!"

Lisa's vocational résumé consists of almost forty years of church and parachurch ministry leadership, including six years as the director of Focus on the Family's national women's ministry, where she created the popular Renewing the Heart conferences, which were attended by almost 200,000 women, as well as a decade of touring with Women of Faith, where she spoke to over a million women about the unconditional love of God. Her academic résumé includes a master of theological studies from Covenant Seminary, and she recently received an earned doctorate from Houston Theological Seminary.

She's been featured on numerous television and radio programs and is a regular on TBN's globally syndicated *Better Together* show, as well as host of *Lisa Harper's Back Porch Theology* podcast, which has surpassed 10 million downloads. She's spoken at hundreds of national and international women's events, as well as in churches around the world. She's also invested locally and has been leading the same weekly neighborhood Bible study for fifteen years. And if you can't find her teaching, studying, hiking, or wakesurfing, she's probably in a coffee shop, sipping a mocha and typing away on her computer because she's also had seventeen books published, including *A Jesus-Shaped Life,* and has written and filmed eleven well-received Bible study video curriculums, including *Luke: A Beautiful Word Bible Study,* which earned the 2024 ECPA Christian Book Award.

However, when asked about her credentials, the most noticeable thing about Lisa Harper is her authenticity. During a recent interview she said, "I'm so grateful for the opportunities God's given me, but don't forget, He often uses donkeys and rocks!" She describes her greatest accomplishment to date as getting to become Missy's mom through the miracle of adoption. In 2014, after a difficult journey and several adoption losses, she finally got to bring her daughter home from Haiti, and she's been smiling even wider ever since.